Seasonal
SANGRIA

101 RECIPES TO ENJOY ALL YEAR LONG!

13-Digit ISBN: 978-1-60433-792-1
10-Digit ISBN: 1-60433-792-3

This book may be ordered by mail from the publisher. Please include $5.99 for postage and handling. Please support your local bookseller first!

Books published by Cider Mill Press Book Publishers are available at special discounts for bulk purchases in the United States by corporations, institutions, and other organizations. For more information, please contact the publisher.

Cider Mill Press Book Publishers
"Where good books are ready for press"
501 Nelson Place
Nashville, Tennessee 37214
cidermillpress.com

Typography: Sentinel, Fenway Park, Bushcraft, Helvetica Rounded

Image Credits: Photos by Zack Bowen: pages 44, 54, 56, 66, 76, 88, 98, 166, 194. All other images used under official license from Shutterstock.com.

Printed in Malaysia

23 24 25 26 27 COS 8 7 6 5 4

Seasonal SANGRIA

101 RECIPES TO ENJOY ALL YEAR LONG!

DOMINIQUE DEVITO

CIDER MILL PRESS

BOOK PUBLISHERS

DEDICATION

Muchas gracias to those whose help with sangria has kept me laughing and sane, and is the only reason I keep coming back for more. Sue Mallen Disy & Andy Monteiro, *con gusto*! The Minks: Karen, Alicia, and Jessie. Bryan VanDeusen, Molly Behrens, MacKenzy Morgan, Dani Palleschi, Caitlin and all the 'Gria Girls, Dylan, Dawson, Jack, Evan, Erin and Grant, and anyone else who helped with Sangria Fest through the years. Trish Rost and Cathe Krueger for chopping, chatting, and helping me come up with the names for these recipes. Jeanne, Betsy, Peter, Lori, and Gene for always being there. And Carlo. Whose idea was this, anyway?

Contents

Sangria's Place In the World and In Your Glass

If you like sangria, you're going to love this book. If you want to like sangria and you're just learning about it, you're going to love this book. If you like wine, and you like fruit, and you like a refreshing drink on a hot day, you're going to love this book. Without proposing any other reasons why, I'm going to tell you flat-out that you're going to love this book. Why? Because it covers everything you need to know about enjoying and making one of the most popular drinks in the world—sangria!

Where It's Been and Where It's Going

Little is known about the origins of sangria. It is speculated that the word derived from the Spanish word for blood—*sangre*—because of its dark red color. The drink is considered quintessentially Spanish, where it's been consumed as a fruit punch consisting of wine, fruits, and brandy for hundreds, if not thousands, of years. It became popular in the United States after being introduced in the Spanish pavilion at the 1964 World's Fair in New York City. Today it is still synonymous with Spain, but is known and enjoyed the world over, and is extremely popular here in the United States.

In Spain, sangria is typically served with a variety of tapas, or little bites of a lot of different foods. It's very versatile that way. Classic Spanish tapas include olives, cheeses, octopus in a spicy sauce, very thin slivers of ham or other meats, garlic, shrimp, mini meatballs, fried chicken livers, so on. You get the idea—salty and spicy foods, and lots of variety. A fruity sangria with a bit of a kick is the perfect complement.

We Americans aren't so bound by custom or tradition. Here, a big bowl of sangria can be the centerpiece of a summer party that goes all night, or it can make for a beautiful and celebratory punch for a luncheon. Making sangria is a good way to use up summer fruit and the inexpensive bottles of wine that get brought over as gifts. A clear pitcher filled with fruit and wine, and smelling of brandy is a welcome sight at any gathering.

One thing to remember when you want sangria to be a part of your party is that while it is very easy to make, it does need time to marinate. Most of the recipes require that the wine, alcohol, and fruit be combined several hours before the sangria be served. You could do this overnight, too. Make room in your party-planning schedule—and in your refrigerator.

This book has 101 recipes for sangria, and if that seems like a lot, well, it is. What you'll learn is that there are many, many combinations that work very well with a variety of wines (more about the best wines later in this chapter). You'll also learn that once you have a basic formula down,

you can mix and match with some confidence. Sangria is fairly formulaic. If you remember the proportions, you will always get it right. They are: one bottle of wine, two cups of juice, syrup and/or soda, a small amount of another liquor, and cut up fruit.

Talking Sangria with The World Wine Guys

When I knew I'd be writing a book about sangria, I consulted The World Wine Guys—Mike DeSimone and Jeff Jenssen. They're legit, not only in matters of wine, but in matters of enjoying wine around the world. They're the entertaining and lifestyle editors at *Wine Enthusiast* magazine; they've written several books about wines from around the world; and—especially important for this book—they live in Spain for part of the year. Who would know more about sangria? We had a great chat about what makes sangria special. The following is a selection of questions I asked them, with their answers. *Gracias*, Mike and Jeff!

We in the United States think of sangria as a quintessentially Spanish drink. Is that true? What is modern-day Spain's relationship to sangria? Sangria is a classic Spanish drink, and at its core it is essentially

what we would refer to as a punch. Although sangria is widely drunk in Spain, it seems to be more popular with tourists than it is with the Spanish. In warm weather, Spaniards drink a "quickie" version of sangria called *tinto verano* or "summer red" that is usually made with un-aged Tempranillo and either lemon soda or a diet lemon-lime soda called La Casera. In Spain we see sangria mainly at traditional restaurants that are popular with visitors and tourists, and also at beach bars on both the Mediterranean and Atlantic coasts.

How would you define a "classic" sangria? Classic sangria is made with red wine, brandy, fruit juice, sugar, and cut fruit. If it is very strong in terms of alcohol—which would be from the brandy—it is diluted with *agua con gas* (sparkling water.)

When do the Spanish drink sangria, and with what? Spaniards usually drink sangria as an aperitif or with tapas. It will be drunk on its own in warm months, especially at outdoor restaurants or beach bars. They will normally just enjoy a bowl of olives and a plate of *jamon* and Manchego cheese with it rather than drink it through an entire meal.

What's your favorite kind of sangria? It's hard to pick just one. We have had the traditional made with red wine, and now white sangria and Cava sangria are popular in Spain, as well. And of course with the rosé craze, we have seen it made with Rosado, too.

What is your favorite occasion for serving sangria? Sangria is a great warm weather party starter. It's very nice to greet guests with an icy glass of just-poured sangria while you are waiting for everyone to arrive.

What are some trends you're seeing with sangria? New flavor combos? Bottled sangria? Sangria made with white wine, rosé or Cava has become popular. With white or Cava, we often see tropical fruit such as pineapple or mango rather than the traditional sliced apples and oranges. Berries are a nice touch, especially frozen blueberries, raspberries, or sliced strawberries. There are some good bottled sangrias on the market that are perfect for the picnic or the beach; there's less fuss and no mixing. Eppa sangria, which is organic, is one of our favorites.

What do you tell people who are making sangria for the first time; i.e., what's most important to keep in mind? Sangria is fairly formulaic; if you remember the proportions you will always get it right. One bottle of wine, two cups of juice, syrup and/or soda, small amount of another liquor, and cut-up fruit. If you are adding brandy or grappa, you might dilute it a little more so things don't get too boozy too fast. And it goes quickly: Have another set of ingredients and a bowl of pre-sliced fruit on hand because you are going to be making a second batch. Better yet, have a third backup ready to go, as well.

Mike DeSimone and Jeff Jenssen, also known as The World Wine Guys, are the entertaining and lifestyle editors at *Wine Enthusiast* magazine and the authors of several books, including *Red Wine* (Sterling Epicure, October 2017.) They divide their time between New York City and Spain.

Sangri-dients

Speaking of what goes into sangria, while it sounds very simple, it can be complex. There are many fruits to choose from, and some go best in red wines and some in white wines. That's been taken into consideration in the chapters, which are divided by red wines, white wines, sparkling wines, sweet wines, and rosé.

Fruit, Fruit and More Fruit!

The recipes in the book feature lots of citrus fruits, including lemons, limes, oranges, and grapefruit.

A variety of stone fruits are excellent in sangrias, including peaches, plums, nectarines, cherries, and apricots.

Did you know apples, pears, and strawberries are pome fruits? They're another member of the rose family (from which stone fruits come).

Berries are must-adds in many sangrias. You can use the cane fruits—blackberries, blueberries, and raspberries—in almost anything.

Tropical fruits are so summery, and no matter the season in which you're enjoying sangria, they can make you feel like you're on a beach in the sun. They include coconut, mango, pineapple, kiwi, passion fruit, and bananas.

Melons work in sangria. Popular ones are watermelon, honeydew, and cantaloupe.

Other fruits that are often used in sangria include grapes, pomegranate, and even figs.

Herbs and Spices

Herbs are typically used to season savory dishes, like rosemary with roasted potatoes, basil in a sauce, or thyme with vegetable and meat dishes. Their savory characteristics also add depth and complexity to cocktails, including sangrias. The recipes in this book include simple syrups and infused vodkas that make use of basil, rosemary, and thyme. Spices that have similar effects that are used in these recipes are chocolate, cinnamon, jalapeño pepper, and lavender.

Spirits and Liqueurs

Authentic sangria includes brandy, which works very well with red wine. Grand Marnier and Triple Sec are orange-flavored brandies and beautifully accentuate sangria's citrus notes. Lighter wines, however, call for spirits that won't clobber the fruits and other flavors, and range from vodka, gin, rum, and even Curacao. There are many flavors of vodka nowadays, and these are fun to add to sangria. Liqueurs can be nice, too. Framboise, Amaretto, Frangelico, St-Germain—what's in your liquor cabinet?

Juices and Sparkling Water

There are so many flavor combinations of juice that I created recipes for what I call "Cheater-Grias"—sangrias that can be quickly and easily assembled because the juices take the place of some of the fresh or frozen fruits, requiring less prep time. There are traditional juices that you'll want to have in your sangri-dients cabinet, including orange juice, pineapple juice, apple juice, white grape juice, and pomegranate juice. There are some more exotic ones that are readily available and delicious, like cherry juice, blueberry juice, and even fig juice. And then there are the combinations. I go into them more in that chapter. There's a staggering amount, so choose what sounds good to you and go for it!

Agua con gas lightens and lifts sangria. Again, we're lucky to be mixing sangrias at a time when there are oodles of flavors of sparkling water. Like anything else, some are better than others. For most of the recipes I recommend plain seltzer. When a sangria features a fruit that needs a little support, I suggest a sparkling water with that flavor, like a watermelon or blueberry seltzer. The more natural the source of the flavor, the better it will taste.

Simple Syrups and Vodka Infusions

For most of the sangria recipes featuring an herb as an ingredient, I give instructions for steeping it in sugar water. A dry red or white wine—or even a dry rosé—needs some sweetener, and the simple syrup accomplishes this. Simple syrup is so easy to make that I always recommend doing it yourself, since the flavor will be so much better. I also suggest making double the amount that's actually used in the sangria. That's because you want to have extra in case you want to increase that flavor. Also, it's nice to see how the flavored simple syrup can embellish other drinks, from adding them to sparkling wine to pouring them over ice and topping with seltzer. Vodka infusions are for sangrias whose base is a sweet wine.

Ahh....the Wines!

Venture into any wine store—even a small one—and there's no denying that wine choices abound. This can be intimidating, so the first thing to remember when choosing a wine to make sangria is to keep it inexpensive. This is not because you want a lousy wine—it shouldn't be downright cheap—but because the wine in sangria is the backdrop, not the centerpiece. You don't have to worry about the wine's subtle flavor profiles complementing your grass-fed roast, you only have to pay (slight) attention to some key attributes, as described below. Also, throughout the book, where I truly feel a particular style will be best suited to the sangria, I've made note of it.

For Red Wines

Reds that are more robust, dry, and with deep fruit notes (but that are not too dry) are the best to pair with more classic, citrus-based sangria. These tend to be wines from Mediterranean and Southern Hemisphere countries, where grapes like Tempranillo, Merlot, and even Cabernet Sauvignon thrive. The World Wine Guys go Spanish in their selection, of course, and defer to Tempranillo and Garnacha for their robust reds. Reds that are lighter but still dry with bright fruit are best for sangrias that feature milder fruits like plums or grapes, or more exotic fruits. These can be inexpensive Beaujolais, California Pinot Noir, lower-priced red blends—almost any dry red $15 and under.

For White Wines

Whites have variations, as well, and fall into two main categories, like reds. These are fruity with a more pronounced mouthfeel (texture/body), and citrusy with a lighter body. If you want a Spanish white, think Albariño, which is dry and light with notes of peach and ripe melon, or Viura, a crisp white from Rioja in Northern Spain. For most white wine sangrias, a simple Pinot Grigio or Sauvignon Blanc works very well, as does Viognier, Gewurztraminer, or a simple Chardonnay.

For Sparkling Wines

I'm of the belief that bubbles do make everything better, and there's something simply joyful about a cold sparkling wine any time of day or year, or in any season. There's no shortage of exceptional, affordable sparkling wines on the market, so here again you have a lot of choice. Don't go Brut (the driest level of sparkling) for a sangria, as you want a bit of residual sugar. Don't go as sweet as something like Asti Spumante, either, as it will mask the fruit flavors. Go for the semi-dry Proseccos, Cavas, or Blanc de Blancs. My advice is to get a mixed case of sparkling and have it on hand for any and all occasions.

For Rosés

These lovely wines, which can be as tasty as they are beautiful, are also plentiful and affordable. You can't go wrong with one that's a middle-of-the-road price point, again, around $15. Spanish rosadas are made with all kinds of grapes, including Tempranillo. The French produce many delicious rosés, and in the United States you can find wonderful rosés coming out of almost every state, but certainly the largest wine producers—California, New York, Washington and Oregon—have you covered.

For Sweet Wines

Most of the recipes for sweet wine suggest a blush. Blush-style wines are pink wines that most of us are used to, as they harken to that pinkest and sweetest and, for a time, trendiest of sweet wines, White Zinfandel. In fact, blush and rosé wines are made in somewhat the same way, using the skins of red wine grapes to affect the color. Before the rosé craze of the past decade or so, Americans tended to think of pink wines as blush, and as sweet. That's how it works for me and for the sangria recipes that call for blush. Any of these recipes can be made with White Zinfandel or one of the sweet pink wines from Barefoot, Sutter, and so on. If you're challenged to find a blush, choose a sweet white like Moscato or go even sweeter with a Riesling. Local wineries tend to feature variations of sweet wines, and they tend to be affordable. Stop in to yours and discover your favorites. All make great sangria.

Sangria Servers

A fruit-laden sangria is as much a visual as a gustatory treat, so be sure to choose a pitcher—or a punch bowl—that will show it off. It's as simple as that. You'll want a ladle handy for serving so you can scoop fruit into each glass.

There is Spanish crockery that's fashioned specifically for sangria, so if you travel to Spain and fall in love with it, be sure to use it when you get home. It's pottery, so you won't be able to see the sangria, but the spout of the pitcher is made with a pinch in the middle to keep just the wine flowing into the glass while keeping the fruit from tumbling out and splashing all over. Using a pitcher like this is great for a more intimate gathering, or perhaps a lunch where you want to feel like you're in sunny Spain.

And there you have it, everything you need to know to get started. Now start making—and enjoying!—sangrias of all styles. Salud!

Many of the pictures in this book feature sprigs of mint as garnish. Mint and other herbs can certainly add a festive and aromatic touch to any sangria, but it's entirely up you!

Red Wine Sangrias

Red wine is the basis for traditional sangria, and so this chapter includes the most recipes. There are so many delicious sangrias made with red wine. Remember, the wine you use for sangria should be—yes!—inexpensive. When making sangria, don't go for that bottle you've put aside to age because you are convinced its complexity will improve the sangria. Instead, it's the fruit and other things you add to the wine you choose that will enable the wine to take on more flavor. Another bonus of sangria!

Red wine has so many fruit notes by its nature—notes of cherry, plum, pomegranate, blackberry, and stewed strawberry, to name a few. All of these can be accentuated and complemented by adding fruits. And, ok, the shot of booze you throw in, the pop of seltzer, and the all-important ice transform a blend of wine and fruit into a delightful punch that tastes better the longer you let it mellow. Just like a great soup. And long kisses. Let's go! *Vamanos*!

The Classic

This is how sangria started, with oranges, apples, and brandy. You can use regular seltzer instead of lemon seltzer, but I like the extra zing the lemon provides. If this is the first sangria you make—and it's a great one to get started with—feel free to improvise to suit your taste. Add more brandy, if you want. Add some sugar, or top with lemon-lime soda instead of seltzer. Remember, sangria should taste good to you. It's a fun, fruity, refreshing wine punch.

Combine all ingredients except the seltzer in a large pitcher or container. Cover and refrigerate for four or more hours. Add ice and seltzer and stir. Serve.

INGREDIENTS

1 bottle (750 ml) dry red wine

2 oranges, sliced thin in whole or half-rounds

2 Granny Smith apples, cored and seeded, cut into bite-sized chunks

¼ cup brandy or Triple Sec

Ice

1 cup lemon seltzer

Classic with a Twist

This sangria throws lemon slices into the basic recipe, and a bit of apple juice to offset the tartness of that fruit. If you're a fan of lemon—the flavor, the color, and the aroma—then this sangria will be more to your liking.

INGREDIENTS

1 bottle (750 ml) dry red wine

2 oranges, sliced into thin rounds, half-rounds, or wedges

1 Granny Smith apple, cored and seeded, cut into bite-sized pieces

1 lemon, sliced into thin rounds, half-rounds, or wedges

2 cups apple juice

¼ cup brandy

Combine all ingredients in a large pitcher or container. Cover and refrigerate for four or more hours. Add ice, stir, and serve.

Classic with a Kick

The brandy that's in sangria adds sweetness and increases the alcohol level. In this recipe, I throw a ¼ cup of apple vodka into the mix. It adds flavor more than sweetness—and a definite kick.

Combine all ingredients except the soda in a large pitcher or container. Cover and refrigerate for four or more hours. Add ice and soda. Stir and serve.

INGREDIENTS

1 bottle (750 ml) dry red wine

1 orange, sliced into thin rounds, half-rounds, or wedges

2 Granny Smith apples, cored and seeded, cut into bite-sized pieces

¼ cup apple vodka

¼ cup brandy

1 12 oz. can lemon-lime soda

Ménage à Trois

YIELD: 4-6 SERVINGS

There are three delicious fruits in this one—oranges, peaches, and grapes—and they get along great in their bath of red wine and peach brandy.

INGREDIENTS

1 bottle (750 ml) dry red wine

2 oranges, sliced thin in whole or half rounds

1 peach, pit removed, cut into thin slices

1 cup red grapes, frozen

¼ cup peach brandy

2 cups seltzer

Combine all ingredients except the seltzer in a large pitcher or container. Cover and refrigerate for four or more hours. Add ice and seltzer. Stir and serve.

Oasis

Make this sangria when you've had a particularly tough week. Its multiple fruits and their layers of flavor are, indeed, an oasis after a stressful workweek.

Combine all ingredients except the seltzer in a large pitcher or container. Cover and refrigerate for four or more hours. Add ice and seltzer. Stir and serve.

INGREDIENTS

1 bottle (750 ml) dry red wine

2 limes, sliced in very thin rounds

1 cup blackberries, frozen

1 cup green grapes, cut in half, frozen

2 cups pomegranate juice

¼ cup brandy

2 cups lemon-lime seltzer

Classic Razz

I love raspberries. The flavor, the color, the texture—everything about them. This is a recipe for classic sangria that has raspberries and raspberry vodka added to it. Yes!

INGREDIENTS

1 bottle (750 ml) dry red wine

2 Granny Smith apples, cored and seeded, cut into bite-sized pieces

1 orange, sliced into thin rounds or half-rounds

1 cup raspberries, frozen

¼ cup raspberry vodka

2 cups seltzer

Combine all ingredients except the seltzer in a large pitcher or container. Cover and refrigerate for four or more hours. Add ice and seltzer. Stir and serve.

Berry Orange-y

If we're playing with berries in a classic sangria, let's try blueberries. The Grand Marnier accentuates the orange flavor, which complements the blueberries perfectly.

1 In a small saucepan, combine blueberries and sugar. Cook over medium heat until blueberries start to burst, about 10 minutes. Allow to simmer, stirring constantly, for another two minutes. Remove from heat and continue to stir occasionally until fruit and sugar are thoroughly combined and slightly cooler.

2 Transfer the blueberry/sugar mixture to a pitcher. Stir in the wine, orange slices, orange juice, and Grand Marnier. Cover and refrigerate for at least four hours.

3 Add ice and seltzer. Stir and serve.

INGREDIENTS

2 cups blueberries

¼ cup sugar

1 cup (750 ml) dry red wine

1 orange, sliced into very thin rounds or half-rounds

1 cup orange juice

¼ cup Grand Marnier

1 cup seltzer

Red Head

With its bouquet of cherries and red grapes, and swimming in red wine, this drink is aptly named the Red Head. As tasty as it is sexy.

INGREDIENTS

1 bottle (750 ml) dry red wine

½ cup sugar

½ cup white grape juice

¼ cup brandy

2 cups cherries

1 cup seedless red grapes, halved and frozen

1 cup seltzer

1 In a large pitcher, add the sugar and white grape juice to the wine, and stir until sugar is dissolved. Add the brandy, cherries, and grapes. Stir, cover the pitcher, and refrigerate for at least four hours.

2 Add seltzer and ice. Stir and serve.

Rum Runner with a Twist

A Rum Runner is a cocktail that features dark rum, and this sangria follows in its footsteps. It's good. Really good. Add up to ¾ cup rum if you're sitting poolside for the rest of the day.

Combine all ingredients in a large pitcher. Cover and refrigerate for at least four hours. Add ice. Stir and serve.

INGREDIENTS

1 bottle (750 ml) dry red wine

2 oranges, cut thin into rounds or half-rounds

2 lemons, cut into very thin rounds

1 lime, cut into very thin half-rounds

1 cup orange juice

½ cup dark rum

Spicy Island

Pineapples and jalapeños—they make a great salsa, so why not a sangria? Give it a try. You'll be happy.

INGREDIENTS

1 bottle (750 ml) dry red wine

1 cup pineapple chunks, frozen

1 jalapeño pepper, seeds removed, sliced thin

1 cup pineapple juice

Dash of hot sauce

2 cups seltzer

Combine all ingredients except the seltzer in a large pitcher. Cover and refrigerate for at least four hours. Add ice and seltzer. Stir and serve.

Summer Day

Strawberries and blueberries—these are the delightful fruits of mid-summer, and they are perfect additions to a red wine sangria. Yes, there are apples, too, and they add texture and color. This is a perfect fruit cocktail for a summer day.

Combine all ingredients except the seltzer in a large pitcher. Cover and refrigerate for at least four hours. Add ice and seltzer. Stir and serve.

INGREDIENTS

1 bottle (750 ml) dry red wine

1 apple, Granny Smith or Empire Red, seeded and cored, cut into bite-sized pieces

1 cup blueberries, frozen

1 cup strawberries, sliced thin and frozen

¼ cup brandy

2 cups non-alcoholic sparkling apple juice or seltzer

Cherry Pom-Pom

This sangria is a lovely combo of dark cherries and pomegranate juice, brightened with lemon. You'll love it.

INGREDIENTS

1 bottle (750 ml) dry red wine

2 cups cherries, pitted, sliced in half

1 lemon, cut into very thin whole slices

1 cup cherry juice

½ cup pomegranate juice

2 cups lemon seltzer

Combine all ingredients except the seltzer in a large pitcher. Cover and refrigerate for at least four hours. Add ice and seltzer. Stir and serve.

Melba Medley

Cherries, yes cherries. And blackberries. And peaches! Peaches bring the other fruits in sync.

Combine all ingredients except the seltzer in a large pitcher. Cover and refrigerate for at least four hours. Add ice and seltzer. Stir and serve.

INGREDIENTS

1 bottle (750 ml) dry red wine

2 cups cherries, pitted, sliced in half

1 cup blackberries

1 peach, pitted, sliced into thin wedges, frozen

½ cup peach vodka

2 cups seltzer

Pear-Fect

A flavor that brings out the greatness of pear is vanilla. The cream soda added to this sangria is the ingredient that makes this pear-grape medley work.

INGREDIENTS

1 bottle (750 ml) dry red wine

2 pears, cored and seeded, cut into chunks

1 cup seedless red grapes, frozen

1 cup orange juice

1 12 oz. can cream soda

Combine all ingredients except the cream soda in a large pitcher. Cover and refrigerate for at least four hours. Add ice and soda. Stir and serve.

Oh My Darlin'

Clementine! Instead of oranges, make a sangria with sweet and seedless clementines. They're offset by the basil, and fortified by the Grand Marnier.

1 Combine wine and sugar in a large pitcher. Stir until sugar is dissolved. Add clementine sections, basil, and Grand Marnier. Cover and refrigerate for at least four hours.

2 Add ice and seltzer. Stir and serve.

INGREDIENTS

1 bottle (750 ml) dry red wine

½ cup sugar

2 clementines, peeled, sections cut in half

6-8 basil leaves, roughly chopped

¼ cup Grand Marnier

2 cups orange seltzer

Cherry Soda Sizzle

Pears and jalapeños jack up this red wine sangria, and the black cherry soda makes it sing.

Combine all ingredients except the soda in a large pitcher. Cover and refrigerate for at least four hours. Add ice and soda. Stir and serve.

INGREDIENTS

1 bottle (750 ml) dry red wine

2 pears, cored and seeded, cut into chunks

1 jalapeño pepper, seeds removed, sliced thin

¼ cup brandy

2 cups black cherry soda

Plumdemonium

Plums taste great marinated in red wine. Add apricots and you've got real depth and layers of flavor.

INGREDIENTS

1 bottle (750 ml) dry red wine

2 plums, pitted and cut into thin wedges, frozen

1 apricot, cut into bite-sized pieces

1 cup cranberry juice

¼ cup brandy

1 cup seltzer

Combine all ingredients except the seltzer in a large pitcher. Cover and refrigerate for at least four hours. Add ice and seltzer. Stir and serve.

Purple Passion

Wait until you see how beautiful the combination of plums, cherries, and blackberries is in your wine glass. It's a "wow" moment.

INGREDIENTS

1 bottle (750 ml) dry red wine

1 plum, pitted and cut into thin wedges, frozen

½ cup cherries, pitted and halved

½ cup blackberries

¼ cup Grand Marnier

2 cups seltzer

Combine all ingredients except the seltzer in a large pitcher. Cover and refrigerate for at least four hours. Add ice and seltzer. Stir and serve.

Variation: Black currants, blueberries, and red grapes also work beautifully in this deep-hued sangria. There should be about two cups of fruit total.

Bough Down

A sangria that piles on the goodness of the orchard—peaches, plums, and apples. Serve this at your apple-picking party!

Combine all ingredients except the soda in a large pitcher. Cover and refrigerate for at least four hours. Add ice and soda. Stir and serve.

INGREDIENTS

1 bottle (750 ml) dry red wine

1 peach, pitted and cut into thin wedges, frozen

1 plum, pitted and cut into thin wedges, frozen

1 Granny Smith apple, cored and seeded, cut into bite-sized pieces

¼ cup brandy

2 cups lemon-lime soda

Cherry Kiss

If you like cherry-flavored sodas—and wines with lovely cherry notes—then you're so going to love this sangria. Oh, and chocolate. Who doesn't like chocolate? This is another sangria that you'll want to make multiple batches of because it'll go fast. Make the simple syrup the day or night before so that it's ready to use when you put the sangria together.

CHOCOLATE SIMPLE SYRUP INGREDIENTS

1 cup water

1 cup sugar

⅓ cup unsweetened cocoa

SANGRIA INGREDIENTS

1 bottle (750 ml) dry red wine

1 cup cherries, pitted and sliced in half

1 12 oz. can black cherry soda

1 Make the chocolate simple syrup: In a small saucepan, combine the water and sugar, and cook, while stirring, over medium heat until the sugar is dissolved. Remove from heat, whisk in the cocoa powder until dissolved, put a lid on the pan, and let the mixture sit for at least three hours. Strain the liquid to remove any cocoa powder residue. Pour syrup into a jar, cover, and refrigerate.

2 When simple syrup is cool, combine ½ to ¾ cup with all ingredients except the soda in a large pitcher. Cover and refrigerate for at least four hours. Add ice and soda. Stir and serve.

Floral on the Finish

Pears are the star of this elegant sangria, which also contains raspberry liqueur and lavender simple syrup. With the seltzer and ice, it's delicious. Garnish with lavender sprigs if desired.

Combine all ingredients except the seltzer in a large pitcher. Cover and refrigerate for at least four hours. Add ice and seltzer. Stir and serve.

INGREDIENTS

1 bottle (750 ml) dry red wine

½ cup lavender simple syrup (see page 83)

2 pears, cored and cut into bite-sized pieces

¼ cup Framboise (raspberry liqueur)

2 cups seltzer

Fall Farmer

When the days get shorter and it's harvest season in the Northeast, apples become the favorite fruit. This sangria is perfect for an Indian Summer day that still has lots of warm sun, but can show off just-picked apples.

INGREDIENTS

1 bottle (750 ml) dry red wine

2 apples, cored and seeded, cut into bite-sized pieces

1 orange, sliced into very thin whole rounds or half-rounds

¼ cup apple vodka

1 cup apple cider

1 dash cinnamon (about ¼ teaspoon)

Pomegranate seeds, for garnish (optional)

Combine all ingredients in a large pitcher. Cover and refrigerate for at least four hours. Add ice. Stir and serve. Garnish with pomegranate seeds if desired.

SERVING SUGGESTION: RIM YOUR GLASS WITH CINNAMON SUGAR FOR A FESTIVE TOUCH! WHOLE PIECES OF CINNAMON ALSO MAKE GREAT SWIZZLE STICKS.

Raspberry Romance

Here's another sangria with chocolate in it, because, well, why not? The results are subtle and surprising and delicious.

INGREDIENTS

2 cups raspberries

½ cup sugar

1 tablespoon unsweetened cocoa powder

1 bottle (750 ml) dry red wine

½ cup chocolate wine

1 cup raspberry sparkling water

1 In a saucepan, combine raspberries and sugar. Cook over medium heat until thoroughly combined, about five minutes, while stirring constantly. Remove from heat and stir to cool slightly. Stir in the unsweetened cocoa powder.

2 In a large pitcher or other container, stir the raspberry/chocolate mixture into the red wine and chocolate wine. Refrigerate for four hours or more. Add ice, stir, and serve.

Get Figgy With It

Figs are a sublime fruit. They are soft and somewhat delicate, which is why they're not in more of these recipes. But they deserve to star in a sangria. They actually have lots of health benefits, too, so if you like the fig juice that should be added to this recipe, you may want to drink it more often.

INGREDIENTS

1 bottle (750 ml) dry red wine

1 cup fresh raspberries

2 or 3 figs, cut into bite-sized pieces, frozen

1 cup fig juice

½ cup pomegranate juice

1 cup seltzer

Sprigs of thyme for garnish

Combine all ingredients except the seltzer in a large pitcher. Cover and refrigerate for at least four hours. Add ice and seltzer. Stir and serve, garnish with thyme.

Flavor Fiesta

This is a "what-the-heck" sangria, featuring a "kitchen sink" combination of fruits, spiked with gin. Give it a try, and play with it to make it your own.

Combine all ingredients except the seltzer in a large pitcher. Cover and refrigerate for at least four hours. Add ice and seltzer. Stir and serve.

INGREDIENTS

1 bottle (750 ml) dry red wine

2 Granny Smith apples, cored and seeded, cut into bite-sized pieces

½ cup mango pieces, frozen

1 cup strawberries, sliced thin and frozen

1 cup white grape juice

¼ cup gin

1 cup seltzer

White Wine Sangrias

While a traditional red wine sangria—with lots of fresh fruit, served over ice, topped with soda or seltzer—can be blissfully refreshing on a hot day (or evening), there's something even more indulgent about a white wine sangria when the temperature rises. White wine cedes to the flavors of fruit with greater ease, making it more of a background ingredient. Because of this, the types of fruits you can use with white wine are more varied. Exotic fruits like mango, watermelon, or kiwi are far more at home in white wine sangria than they are in the red wine version. White wine is also a great medium for herb- and flower-infused simple syrups, which complement many fruits. By steeping herbs and fruits in the syrup, you get all the flavor while keeping the sangria from being too herbaceous or sharp.

The fruits are also more aesthetically pleasing in a white wine sangria. After fruit has marinated in red wine, it turns, well, purple. It tastes great, but it looks bruised. This doesn't happen to the fruit in white wine sangria (though it will soften and discolor somewhat if left in the wine for more than a day). A glass of white wine sangria is an aqueous still life. Beautiful. And delicious.

The same basic rules apply for the selection of an appropriate white wine as for a red. Because you'll be adding fruit, juice, spirits, and possibly soda or seltzer, you don't want to sacrifice your California wine club selection of the month. What you want is something simple and inexpensive. Do try to avoid "cheap" wine, because it's likely to contribute little or nothing to the taste, and give you and your guests headaches. There are lots of great choices in the $12 to $20 range.

White wine flavors broadly fall into the categories of citrusy, steely, buttery, and minerally. Each of these will complement fruits in a different way. Something buttery, like an oak-aged Chardonnay, will show off the tropical notes in pineapple or honeydew melon, whereas a minerally, bright white like a French Chablis is especially suited to the crisp flavors of apple or the lusciousness of blackberries. But there's no need to overthink your selection. The recipes here will work with whatever style suits you best. If I think there's a wine that would work especially well in the recipe, I recommend it, but it's by no means a requirement.

Remember, sangria is forgiving. It's a celebration of fruit and flavor that's best shared with good friends and good food.

Sangria Blanca

If you want to go as basic as possible, this is a good white wine sangria to start with. The different colored grapes look great in the glass, the white grape juice adds a pleasant sweetness, and of course there's brandy and bubbles.

INGREDIENTS

1 bottle (750 ml) dry white wine

1 cup seedless green grapes, halved

½ cup seedless red grapes, halved

2 cups white grape juice

¼ cup brandy

2 cups seltzer

Combine all ingredients except the seltzer in a large pitcher or container. Cover and refrigerate for four or more hours. Add ice and seltzer. Stir and serve.

Sweet Peach

The flavor of peaches is fabulous in red or white wine, but the pieces look especially nice in a glass of white wine—especially alongside blueberries!

Combine all ingredients except the seltzer in a large pitcher or container. Cover and refrigerate for four or more hours. Add ice and seltzer. Stir and serve.

INGREDIENTS

1 bottle (750 ml) dry white wine

2 peaches, pits removed, cut into bite-sized pieces

½ cup blueberries, frozen

1 cup peach nectar

¼ cup peach schnapps

2 cups seltzer

Lemon-Lime Time

YIELD: 4-6 SERVINGS

On a really hot day, there's nothing like the bright pop of citrus—oranges, lemons, and limes. They give a dry, light-bodied white wine a whole other level of freshness. Top the glasses with those cute paper umbrellas for a real party feel.

INGREDIENTS

1 bottle (750 ml) dry white wine

1 large orange, sliced into quarter-moon slivers

½ lemon, sliced into half-moon slivers

½ lime, sliced into half-moon slivers

¼ cup Triple Sec

2 cups lemon-lime soda

Combine all ingredients except the soda in a large pitcher or container. Cover and refrigerate for four or more hours. Add ice and soda. Stir and serve.

Juicy Melon

This one's called a Juicy Melon because it combines orange juice with honeydew melon. Since the Midori is essential to this one, adding seltzer instead of flavored soda keeps the sangria from being too sweet.

Combine all ingredients except the seltzer in a large pitcher or container. Cover and refrigerate for four or more hours. Add ice and seltzer. Stir and serve.

INGREDIENTS

1 bottle (750 ml) dry white wine

1 large orange, sliced into quarter-moon slivers

1 cup honeydew melon, cut into bite-sized pieces

½ cup Midori melon liqueur

2 cups seltzer

Coco-Loco

What's nice about this one is that the pear and mango are very complementary. They balance the strong taste of coconut because they're not super-sweet themselves. If you stir this up and it's not sweet enough for you, add more coconut cream, one teaspoon at a time.

Combine all ingredients except the seltzer in a large pitcher or container. Cover and refrigerate for four or more hours. Add ice and seltzer. Stir and serve.

INGREDIENTS

1 bottle (750 ml) dry white wine

1 cup frozen mango pieces, bite-sized

1 cup frozen pear pieces, bite-sized

½ cup coconut cream

½ cup coconut vodka

2 cups seltzer

Berry Blue

So named because this sangria is loaded with fresh summer berries—raspberries, blackberries, and blueberries. Throw in the berry-flavored vodka and the raspberry juice, and you have a berry tasty sangria!

INGREDIENTS

1 bottle (750 ml) dry white wine

½ cup raspberries, frozen

½ cup blackberries, frozen

½ cup blueberries, frozen

½ cup berry vodka

1 cup raspberry juice

2 cups seltzer

Combine all ingredients except the seltzer in a large pitcher or container. Cover and refrigerate for four or more hours. Add ice and seltzer. Stir and serve.

Lavender Lift

Lavender adds a subtle floral note to beverages and foods. Have you ever had lavender ice cream? It's amazing! If this is your first experience with lavender-infused simple syrup, you're in for a treat. If it's not, you know what's possible. Make the simple syrup the day or the night before so it's ready when you want to put the sangria together.

1 Make the lavender simple syrup: In a small saucepan, combine the water and sugar. Cook, while stirring, over medium heat until the sugar is dissolved. Add the lavender sprigs or flowers. Remove from heat and cover the saucepan. Steep the lavender in the sugar water for two hours. Remove the sprigs and/or strain the flowers from the syrup. Pour the lavender-infused simple syrup into a small jar and refrigerate. The syrup will keep in the refrigerator, tightly sealed, for up to two weeks.

2 Combine the wine, gin or vodka, fruits, and 1 cup of the lavender simple syrup in a large pitcher or container. Cover and refrigerate for four or more hours. Add ice and seltzer. Stir and serve, garnishing glasses with sprigs of lavender if desired.

LAVENDER SIMPLE SYRUP INGREDIENTS

1 cup sugar

1 cup water

4 sprigs fresh lavender or 2 tablespoons dried lavender flowers

SANGRIA INGREDIENTS

1 bottle (750 ml) dry white wine

¼ cup gin or vodka

1 cup blueberries, frozen

1 kiwi, peeled, frozen, and cut into bite-sized pieces

1½ cups blueberry seltzer

Sprigs of lavender for garnish

Melon Marvel

Pairing the sweetness of watermelon with a hint of licorice from the basil makes this one a doozy! Make the simple syrup the day or night before so it's ready when you want to put the sangria together.

BASIL SIMPLE SYRUP INGREDIENTS

1 cup sugar

1 cup water

¼ cup fresh basil leaves

SANGRIA INGREDIENTS

1 bottle (750 ml) dry white wine

2 cups frozen watermelon pieces, bite-sized

1 cup watermelon seltzer or 1 cup watermelon juice and 1 cup plain seltzer

Fresh basil leaves for garnish, if desired

Lime slices for garnish, if desired

1 Make the basil-infused simple syrup: In a small saucepan, combine the water and sugar. Cook, while stirring, over medium heat until the sugar is dissolved. Add the basil leaves. Remove from heat and cover the saucepan. Steep the basil in the syrup for two hours. Remove the leaves and pour the syrup into a small jar. Refrigerate. The syrup will keep in the refrigerator, tightly sealed, for up to two weeks.

2 Combine the wine, fruits, and 1 cup of the simple syrup in a large pitcher or container. Cover and refrigerate for four or more hours. Add ice and seltzer. Stir and serve, garnishing glasses with basil leaves if desired.

Variations: This recipe is equally delicious when made with mint simple syrup, or by adding other melon varieties, such as cantaloupe or honeydew.

Piña-Gria

There's no arguing with the great taste of a piña colada—a rum drink bursting with coconut and pineapple. Here it is in sangria form. If you want to enhance the coconut flavor, add more cream of coconut, one teaspoon at a time.

Combine all ingredients except the seltzer in a large pitcher or container. Cover and refrigerate for four or more hours. Add ice and seltzer. Stir and serve.

INGREDIENTS

1 bottle (750 ml) dry white wine (oaked Chardonnay is especially good for this one)

1 cup frozen pineapple pieces, bite-sized

1 cup pineapple juice

½ cup cream of coconut

½ cup coconut vodka

1 cup seltzer

Sassy & Savory

Grapefruit, blueberry, and rosemary—these aren't ingredients for those hankering for something sweet, but it is a great combo for a super-refreshing summer quencher. Make the simple syrup the day or night before so it's ready when you want to put the sangria together.

SIMPLE SYRUP INGREDIENTS

½ cup water

½ cup sugar

SANGRIA INGREDIENTS

1 bottle (750 ml) dry white wine

1 grapefruit, peeled and seeded, sections cut into thirds

2 cups blueberries, frozen

¼ cup grapefruit vodka

4-6 sprigs fresh rosemary

2 cups seltzer

1 Make the simple syrup: Combine the water and sugar in a small saucepan and cook, while stirring, over medium heat until sugar is dissolved. Allow syrup to cool slightly, then transfer to a bowl or jar and refrigerate for at least a half-hour before using. The syrup will keep in the refrigerator, tightly sealed, for up to two weeks.

2 Combine all ingredients except the seltzer and rosemary sprigs in a large pitcher or container. Cover and refrigerate for four or more hours. Add ice and seltzer. Stir and serve with sprigs of rosemary in the glasses.

Black-Eyed Peach

When you see the blackberries peeking around the peach pieces in this colorful and delicious sangria, you'll understand how it got its name.

Combine all ingredients except the seltzer in a large pitcher or container. Cover and refrigerate for four or more hours. Add ice and seltzer. Stir and serve.

INGREDIENTS

1 bottle (750 ml) dry white wine

1 large or 2 medium peaches, pitted and cut into bite-sized pieces, frozen

½ cup blackberries

1 cup peach nectar

¼ cup peach schnapps

2 cups seltzer

Honey Plum

There are so many flavored vodkas, and any of them can enhance a fruity sangria. For this one, the vodka chosen is a honey vodka, so it provides a nice note of sweetness without overdoing it.

INGREDIENTS

1 bottle (750 ml) dry white wine

1 nectarine, pitted and cut into bite-sized pieces, frozen

2 plums, pitted and cut into bite-sized pieces, frozen

½ cup honey vodka

1 12 oz. can lemon-lime soda

Combine all ingredients except the soda in a large pitcher or container. Cover and refrigerate for four or more hours. Add ice and soda. Stir and serve.

Sí Señor

Many of the sangrias in this book feature exotic ingredients. This one features a more traditional combo of fruits, so I dubbed it Sí Señor.

Combine all ingredients except the seltzer in a large pitcher or container. Cover and refrigerate for four or more hours. Add ice and seltzer. Stir and serve.

INGREDIENTS

1 bottle (750 ml) dry white wine

1 cup seedless red grapes, halved

1 Granny Smith apple, cored and seeded, cut into bite-sized pieces

½ orange, cut into half-moon slivers

2 cups apple juice (not cider)

½ cup brandy

2 cups seltzer

Sí Señora

A variation on the Sí Señor (page 95), but with fruits that are a bit sweeter and more—dare I say?—feminine!

INGREDIENTS

1 bottle (750 ml) dry white wine

1 cup seedless green grapes, halved

2 white peaches, pitted, cut into bite-sized pieces

2 cups white grape juice

½ cup peach vodka

2 cups seltzer

Combine all ingredients except the seltzer in a large pitcher or container. Cover and refrigerate for four or more hours. Add ice and seltzer. Stir and serve.

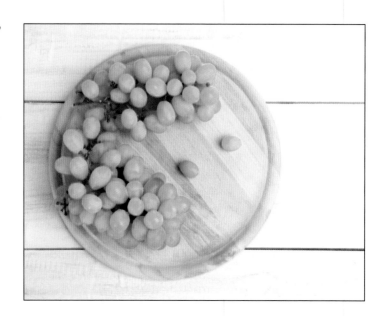

Blue Dew

If you want a white wine sangria that's neon green, has floating bits of light green and blue, smells amazing—and tastes darn good, too—then give this one a try. Picture yourself poolside if you're unsure about trying it.

Combine all ingredients except the seltzer in a large pitcher or container. Cover and refrigerate for four or more hours. Add ice and seltzer. Stir and serve.

INGREDIENTS

1 bottle (750 ml) dry white wine

1½ cups honeydew melon, cut into bite-sized pieces

1 cup blueberries, frozen

½ cup Midori melon liqueur

2 cups seltzer

Trouble in the Tropics

YIELD: 4-6 SERVINGS

How can there be trouble in the tropics? By introducing more heat—in this case, in the form of a jalapeño. The effect of the fiery pepper in the drink is that you taste fruit up front, but get fire on the finish.

Combine all ingredients except the soda in a large pitcher or container. Cover and refrigerate for four or more hours. Add ice and soda. Stir and serve.

INGREDIENTS

1 bottle (750 ml) dry white wine (an oaked Chardonnay is especially good with this)

1 cup frozen pineapple pieces, bite-sized

1 fresh jalapeño pepper, sliced thin (wear gloves to cut the pepper)

1 12 oz. can lemon-lime soda

Pepper Peach

In this sangria, that same jalapeño that led to trouble in the tropics brings its pizzazz to peaches and mango. The result is oh so flavorful.

INGREDIENTS

1 bottle (750 ml) dry white wine (an oaked Chardonnay is especially good with this)

½ cup frozen mango pieces, bite-sized

1 fresh jalapeño pepper, sliced thin (wear gloves to cut the pepper)

1 large peach, pitted, cut into bite-sized pieces, frozen

2 cups peach juice

1 cup seltzer

Combine all ingredients except the seltzer in a large pitcher or container. Cover and refrigerate for four or more hours. Add ice and seltzer. Stir and serve.

Sleek Heat

Grapes and plums are enhanced by the tangy fire of a ginger-infused simple syrup in this sangria—which is as pretty as it is tasty. If you want something sweeter, substitute ginger ale for seltzer. Make the simple syrup the day or night before so it's ready when you want to put the sangria together.

1 Make the ginger-infused simple syrup: In a small saucepan, combine the sugar and water. Cook over medium heat, while stirring, until sugar is dissolved. Add the fresh ginger slices. Remove from the heat and cover, letting the ginger steep for about two hours. Remove the slices and strain the syrup into a jar to remove any pulp. Cover and refrigerate. The syrup will keep in the refrigerator, tightly sealed, for up to two weeks.

2 Combine ½ cup simple syrup with all ingredients except the seltzer in a large pitcher or container. Cover and refrigerate for four or more hours. Add ice and seltzer. Stir and serve.

GINGER SIMPLE SYRUP INGREDIENTS

1 cup sugar

1 cup water

1 piece fresh ginger root, peeled and sliced thin

SANGRIA INGREDIENTS

1 bottle (750 ml) dry white wine

1 cup seedless green grapes, halved and frozen

2 plums, pitted and cut into bite-sized pieces, frozen

1 cup seltzer

Fall Fruit Fiesta

Apples and grapes, a splash of lime, and a bath of delicious pomegranate juice give you a sangria that will disappear in no time.

Combine all ingredients except the soda in a large pitcher or container. Cover and refrigerate for four or more hours. Add ice and soda. Stir and serve.

SERVING SUGGESTION: RIM YOUR GLASS WITH CINNAMON SUGAR FOR A FESTIVE TOUCH! WHOLE PIECES OF CINNAMON ALSO MAKE GREAT SWIZZLE STICKS.

INGREDIENTS

1 bottle (750 ml) dry white wine

1 Red Delicious or Empire apple, cored, cut into bite-sized pieces

1 cup seedless green grapes, halved

1 cup pomegranate juice

Juice of 1 lime

¼ cup brandy

1 12 oz. can lemon-lime soda

Pomegranate seeds, for garnish

Lemon Thyme

YIELD: 4-6 SERVINGS

Lemon thyme is actually an herb unto itself, but it's very subtle. To reap the full rewards of this great (and natural) flavor combo in a sangria, it's better to make a thyme-infused simple syrup and mix it with fresh lemon and some lemon liqueur. Garnish the glasses with sprigs of thyme for a beautiful presentation. Make the simple syrup the day or night before so it's ready when you want to put the sangria together.

THYME SIMPLE SYRUP INGREDIENTS

1 cup sugar

1 cup water

4 sprigs fresh thyme or 1 tablespoon dried thyme

SANGRIA INGREDIENTS

1 bottle (750 ml) dry white wine

1 lemon, sliced into very thin quarter-moon slivers

½ cup Limoncello or other lemon liqueur

2 cups seltzer

4-6 sprigs of thyme for garnish

1 Make the thyme-infused simple syrup: In a small saucepan, combine the sugar and water. Cook over medium heat, while stirring, until sugar is dissolved. Add the sprigs or dried thyme. Remove from the heat and cover the saucepan. Leave for two hours. Remove the sprigs and/or strain out the herbs, and pour the syrup into a small jar. Cover and refrigerate. The syrup will keep in the refrigerator, tightly sealed, for up to two weeks.

2 Once cooled, combine ½ cup of the simple syrup with all remaining ingredients except the seltzer in a large pitcher or container. Cover and refrigerate for four or more hours. Add ice and seltzer. Stir and serve, garnishing with thyme sprigs if desired.

Berry Banilla

Isn't that a cute name? If you love notes of vanilla—which are often in oaked whites, like buttery California chardonnays—then you'll love this sangria. The pears and blueberries complement the vanilla perfectly, and the cream soda adds a wonderful finishing touch.

Combine all ingredients except the soda in a large pitcher or container. Cover and refrigerate for two hours. Remove the vanilla bean and refrigerate for two more hours. Add ice and soda. Stir and serve.

INGREDIENTS

1 bottle (750 ml) dry white wine (a light white is best for this, like a Sauvignon Blanc)

2 pears, cored and seeded, cut into bite-sized pieces and frozen

1 cup blueberries, frozen

1 whole vanilla bean

½ cup vanilla vodka

1 12 oz. can cream soda

Spring Fling

Strawberries and rhubarb are associated with spring, at least in the Northeast where I grew up. They're a treasured pairing coming off a long winter, with the sweetness of strawberries and the fresh acidity of rhubarb. They can be paired in sangria, too. Make the simple syrup the day or night before so it's ready when you want to put the sangria together.

RHUBARB SIMPLE SYRUP INGREDIENTS

1 cup water

1 cup sugar

1 cup rhubarb pieces

SANGRIA INGREDIENTS

1 bottle (750 ml) dry white wine

2 cups strawberries, cut into bite-sized pieces

¼ cup vodka

1 cup plain seltzer

1 Make the rhubarb simple syrup: Combine the water and sugar in a small saucepan. Cook over medium heat, while stirring, until sugar is dissolved. Add the rhubarb pieces and stir. Remove from heat and allow to steep for at least two hours. Remove the rhubarb and strain the syrup into a jar to remove any strands from the fruit. Cover the jar and refrigerate. The syrup will keep in the refrigerator, tightly sealed, for up to two weeks.

2 Combine 1 cup of the simple syrup with all remaining ingredients except the seltzer in a large pitcher or container. Cover and refrigerate for four or more hours. Add ice and seltzer. Stir and serve.

Scheherazade

Scheherazade is the female storyteller in *One Thousand and One Nights*, an ancient Persian manuscript. She kept a man from killing her by telling a story so beguiling that he had to keep listening night after night. This sangria will have you coming back for more of its exotic nature, and that's a promise.

Combine all ingredients except the seltzer in a large pitcher or container. Cover and refrigerate for four or more hours. Add ice and seltzer. Stir and serve.

INGREDIENTS

1 bottle (750 ml) dry white wine

1 Granny Smith apple, cored and cut into bite-sized pieces

1 cup fresh cherries, pitted and halved, frozen

½ cup Frangelico or hazelnut liqueur

1 cup seltzer

Berry'd Alive

I like the big taste of blackberries in this sangria, but blueberries would be fine, too. The strawberries are essential.

INGREDIENTS

1 bottle (750 ml) dry white wine

1½ cup chopped strawberries

1 cup blackberries

2 cups blueberry-pomegranate juice

½ cup berry-flavored vodka

1 cup berry-flavored seltzer

Combine all ingredients except the seltzer in a large pitcher or container. Cover and refrigerate for four or more hours. Add ice and seltzer. Stir and serve.

Choco-Nana-Gria

A chocolate-banana sangria? Yes! Your guests will be surprised and delighted by this treat. The chocolate-infused simple syrup is really fun. If it's not sweet enough for you, add a quarter cup of a basic chocolate wine, which you can find in any liquor store.

CHOCOLATE SIMPLE SYRUP INGREDIENTS

1 cup sugar

1 cup water

⅓ cup unsweetened cocoa powder

SANGRIA INGREDIENTS

1 bottle (750 ml) dry white wine

1 large, ripe but firm banana, cut into thin slices

¼ cup chocolate vodka (or plain if you can't find it)

1 cup seltzer

1 Make the chocolate-infused simple syrup: In a small saucepan, combine the sugar and water. Cook over medium heat, while stirring, until the sugar is dissolved. Stir in the cocoa powder until well blended. Remove from heat, cover, and let sit for about an hour. Strain the syrup into a jar, using a fine mesh strainer to remove as much of the powder as possible. Cover and refrigerate.

2 Combine all ingredients except the seltzer in a large pitcher or container. Cover and refrigerate for two or more hours. Add ice and seltzer. Stir and serve.

Sparkling Wine Sangrias

There's a saying in my house: Bubbles make everything better. It refers specifically to champagne. There's nothing that can clear the cobwebs and restore a sense of joy better than a glass of cold champagne, with its lovely little bubbles dancing up the side of a glass and a slightly yeasty nose that's as intoxicating as fresh-baked bread. As delightful as a glass of bubbly is on its own, it can also transform any ingredients to which it's added. Think of the classic Mimosa, which is simply champagne and orange juice. Or the Bellini, which is champagne and peach juice. Or the Black Velvet, an inspired combo of equal parts champagne and a dark Porter beer. You get the idea.

In this chapter, all the sangria recipes are topped with champagne. There's just no going wrong. No, wait, you could go slightly wrong. While classic sangria recipes call for inexpensive wine as the base, with the bubbly sangrias you need to be a bit more discriminating. Not that you should be adding Moët Chandon to the sangrias—that's overkill—but neither should you be using a sweet Asti Spumante. That's overkill to the other extreme, resulting in a sangria that's too sweet. The best choice of bubbly for these sangrias is a mid-range sparkling wine. Types of wine are discussed more fully in the Sangri-dients chapter, so if you need a refresher on the types of sparkling wine and what's best, refer back to that. But make sure you choose something on the drier side.

Berry Bubbly

This is a delightful summertime sparkling sangria that's rife with fresh strawberries and blueberries. A perfect occasion? A sangria toast on the 4th of July.

INGREDIENTS

1 cup sliced frozen strawberries, thawed, juice reserved

1 cup blueberries, frozen

1 tablespoon fresh-squeezed lime juice

1 bottle (750 ml) sparkling wine, very cold

1 In a bowl, combine the thawed strawberries, their juice, and the blueberries. Stir. Sprinkle the fruit with the lime juice and fold the fruits lightly.

2 In 4-6 glasses, ladle two spoonfuls of fruit. Top each glass with sparkling wine. Repeat as desired with any remaining fruit and wine, making sure to keep the wine chilled.

Peachy Keen

This is another sangria that is perfect for summer, and should be made as often as possible during peach season, when the fruit is simply succulent.

1 In a bowl, combine the peach pieces, blueberries, and schnapps. Stir to combine.

2 In 4-6 glasses, ladle two spoonfuls of fruit. Top each glass with sparkling wine. Repeat as desired with any remaining fruit and wine, making sure to keep the wine chilled.

INGREDIENTS

1 cup bite-sized peach pieces (skin on is fine)

1 cup blueberries, frozen

¼ cup peach schnapps

1 bottle (750 ml) sparkling wine, very cold

Hello, Honey!

The combination of red and green grapes with the melon pieces makes for a lovely visual presentation, especially when the bubbles from the sparkling wine are dancing on the fruit. The hint of melon liqueur takes this one over the top.

INGREDIENTS

½ cup seedless red grapes, cut in half

½ cup seedless green grapes, cut in half

1 cup honeydew melon pieces, bite-sized

2 tablespoons Midori liqueur

1 bottle (750 ml) sparkling wine, very cold

1 In a bowl, combine the grape halves and melon pieces. Sprinkle with the Midori and fold so that the fruit is covered with the liqueur.

2 In 4-6 glasses, ladle two spoonfuls of fruit. Top each glass with sparkling wine. Repeat as desired with any remaining fruit and wine, making sure to keep the wine chilled.

Fruity Down Under

This sangria is wonderful as is. But if you're looking to take it up a notch, spike it with a liquor cabinet staple—gin! Its slight tanginess goes well with the watermelon and kiwi.

1 In a food processor or blender, puree the large watermelon pieces with the sugar until the melon is pulverized into sweetened juice.

2 Pour the watermelon juice in a bowl, and add the bite-sized pieces of watermelon and kiwi. Stir to combine.

3 In 4-6 glasses, ladle two spoonfuls of fruit and two spoonfuls of the juice. Top each glass with sparkling wine. Repeat as desired with any remaining fruit and juice, making sure to keep the wine chilled.

INGREDIENTS

2 cups large watermelon pieces

¼ cup sugar

1 cup bite-sized watermelon pieces, frozen

½ cup bite-sized kiwi pieces, frozen

1 bottle (750 ml) sparkling wine, very cold

Nutty Cherry

This sangria features fruit that's as colorful as it is tasty—deep red cherries and orange nectarines. Their flavors are highlighted by a helping of hazelnut liqueur.

INGREDIENTS

1 cup cherries, pitted and halved (fresh only)

1 cup bite-sized fresh nectarine pieces

¼ cup Amaretto or hazelnut liqueur

1 bottle (750 ml) sparkling wine, very cold

1 In a bowl, combine the cherry and nectarine pieces. Pour the Amaretto over them. Cover with plastic wrap and marinate the fruit in the refrigerator for at least two hours, and up to six hours.

2 In 4-6 glasses, ladle two spoonfuls of fruit/liqueur. Top each glass with sparkling wine. Repeat as desired with any remaining fruit, making sure to keep the wine chilled.

Black London

This sangria is all about presentation. Rather than mix the fruit and beverages in a pitcher together, the fruits are divided among the glasses, which are then topped with a lemon/gin cocktail and the sparkling wine.

1 In a measuring cup, combine the fresh-squeezed lemon juice and gin. Stir well to combine.

2 In 4-6 glasses, place two blackberries and one raspberry. Pour an equal amount of the lemon/gin mixture into each glass. Top each glass with sparkling wine. Add more cold wine over the fruit as desired.

INGREDIENTS

½ cup fresh-squeezed lemon juice, all seeds removed

¼ cup gin

12 fresh blackberries

6 fresh raspberries

1 bottle (750 ml) sparkling wine, very cold

Hot Tropixx

If you're in the mood for a tropical sangria, made all the more appealing by sparkling wine, then this one is for you. There's even a hint of heat from the jalapeño to get your heart pumping.

INGREDIENTS

1 cup bite-sized pieces of fresh pineapple

¾ cup diced mangos from a 15 oz. can

½ cup juice from the can of diced mangos

1 jalapeño pepper, sliced thin (wear gloves to cut the hot pepper)

¼ cup fresh-squeezed lime juice

¼ cup vodka

1 bottle (750 ml) sparkling wine, very cold

1 In a bowl, combine the pineapple pieces, diced mango, mango juice, jalapeño, lime juice, and vodka. Cover and refrigerate for up to two hours. After two hours, strain the juice into a measuring cup.

2 In 4-6 glasses, ladle two spoonfuls of fruit. Pour equal amounts of the mango/lime juice into each glass. Top each glass with sparkling wine, continuing to top the glass as desired.

Apple & Spice

After you've gone apple picking, you want to make a fun drink to enjoy while you prepare an apple pie. Throw this sangria together—the dash of nutmeg is just the right touch.

1 In a bowl, combine the apple pieces and cranberries. Pour the cranberry juice, apple cider, and apple vodka over the fruits. Add the dash of nutmeg and stir to combine. Cover and refrigerate for at least two hours, and up to six hours. Then remove from refrigerator and strain the juice into a measuring cup.

2 In 4-6 glasses, ladle two spoonfuls of fruit. Pour equal amounts of the juice/vodka combination into each glass and top with sparkling wine, refilling as necessary.

INGREDIENTS

1 Granny Smith apple, cored, seeded, peeled, and cut into bite-sized pieces

1 Empire apple, cored, seeded, peeled, and cut into bite-sized pieces

½ cup fresh cranberries

¼ cup cranberry juice

¼ cup apple cider

¼ cup apple vodka

Dash of nutmeg

1 bottle (750 ml) sparkling wine, very cold

Thyme on the Farm

The thyme-infused simple syrup adds a subtle flavor to the berries and melon. It's so refreshing!

INGREDIENTS

1 cup fresh strawberries, sliced thin

½ cup bite-sized honeydew melon pieces

½ cup thyme simple syrup (see page 104)

¼ cup vodka

1 bottle (750 ml) sparkling wine, very cold

4-6 sprigs of thyme for garnish

1 In a bowl, combine the strawberries and melon pieces. Add the simple syrup and vodka. Cover and refrigerate for about an hour.

2 Divide the fruit/syrup mixture between 4-6 glasses. Top each glass with the wine, adding more as desired.

Wacky Watermelon Basil

If this sounds like an odd combination, well, it is—but it works! The slight licorice notes from the basil work really well with the watermelon.

1 In a bowl, combine the apple and watermelon pieces. Pour the simple syrup and vodka on top and stir to combine. Cover the bowl and refrigerate for at least two hours, and up to six hours. When ready to remove from refrigerator, strain the juice into a measuring cup.

2 In 4-6 glasses, ladle two spoonfuls of fruit. Pour equal amounts of the liquid into each glass and top with the sparkling wine.

INGREDIENTS

1 large Granny Smith apple, cored, seeded, peeled, and cut into bite-sized pieces

1 cup bite-sized fresh watermelon pieces

½ cup basil-infused simple syrup (see page 84)

¼ cup watermelon vodka

1 bottle (750 ml) sparkling wine, very cold

Berry Provençal

Ah, to be in the south of France looking out over fields of lavender in the Mediterranean sunshine! If you can't get there, at least you can pretend when you have this sangria.

LAVENDER SIMPLE SYRUP INGREDIENTS

1 cup water

1 cup sugar

4 sprigs or 2 tablespoons dried lavender flowers

SANGRIA INGREDIENTS

1 pint raspberries, frozen

1 cup blueberries, frozen

¾ cup lavender simple syrup

1 bottle (750 ml) sparkling wine, very cold

1 Make the lavender simple syrup: In a small saucepan, combine the water and sugar. Cook, stirring, over medium heat until the sugar is dissolved. Add the lavender sprigs or flowers. Remove from heat and cover the saucepan. Steep the lavender in the sugar water for about 2 hours. Remove the sprigs and/or strain the flowers from the sugar water. Pour the lavender-infused simple syrup into a small jar and refrigerate. The syrup will keep in a sealed jar in the refrigerator for several weeks.

2 In a bowl, combine the raspberries and blueberries. Add the lavender simple syrup. Cover and refrigerate for about an hour.

3 Divide the fruit/syrup mixture into 4 to 6 glasses or champagne flutes. Top each glass with sparkling wine, refilling as necessary.

Green With Envy

You could build a whole meal around this green-themed sangria. Even if you don't, this one is sure to bring repeat visitors to your parties.

1 Make the rosemary simple syrup: Remove the needles from sprigs of fresh rosemary until you have ¼ cup. In a small saucepan, combine water, sugar, and the rosemary needles. Bring the mixture to a boil over medium heat, stirring to dissolve the sugar. Once it's at a boil, reduce the heat to low and let the syrup simmer for just a minute or two. Remove from the heat and cover the saucepan. Steep the syrup for about 20 minutes. Strain the cooled syrup into an airtight glass container and refrigerate. The syrup will keep, refrigerated, for about 3 weeks.

2 In a bowl, combine the apple and grape pieces. Add ½ cup of the rosemary simple syrup, white grape juice, and apple vodka. Cover and refrigerate for at least two hours, and up to six hours. When ready to remove from refrigerator, strain the juice into a measuring cup.

3 In 4-6 glasses, ladle two spoonfuls of the fruit. Divide the juice/syrup equally among the glasses, and top each with sparkling wine. Refill as necessary.

ROSEMARY SIMPLE SYRUP INGREDIENTS

¼ cup sprigs fresh rosemary

1 cup water

1 cup sugar

SANGRIA INGREDIENTS

2 Granny Smith apples, cored, seeded, and cut into bite-sized pieces

½ cup seedless green grapes, cut in half, frozen

½ cup white grape juice

¼ cup apple vodka

1 bottle (750 ml) sparkling wine, very cold

Blackened Pear

Pepper isn't just for savory dishes—it adds a note of spice and intrigue to fruity and sweet dishes and drinks, too. Go ahead, give it a try.

BLACK PEPPER SIMPLE SYRUP INGREDIENTS

1½ cups water

1 cup sugar

1 tablespoon black peppercorns, whole

1 tablespoon black peppercorns, coarsely ground

SANGRIA INGREDIENTS

1 cup diced pear pieces from a 15 oz. can

¼ cup juice from the can of pear pieces

12 blackberries, plus more for garnish

1 bottle (750 ml) sparkling wine, very cold

1 Make the black pepper simple syrup: In a small saucepan, combine water, sugar, whole black peppercorns, and coarsely ground black peppercorns. Bring the mixture to a boil over medium heat, stirring to dissolve the sugar. Once it's at a boil, reduce the heat to low and let the syrup simmer for 15-20 minutes. Remove from the heat and allow to cool. Strain the cooled syrup into an airtight glass container and refrigerate. The syrup will keep, refrigerated, for about 3 weeks.

2 In a bowl, combine the pear pieces, juice from the pears, blackberries, and ¼ cup black pepper simple syrup. Cover and refrigerate for about an hour.

3 Divide the fruits and juices between 4-6 glasses. Top each glass with sparkling wine and any remaining blackberries.

Orange You Pretty

If you need a burst of color in your glass, this is the sangria for you. And it tastes, well, amazing!

1 In a bowl, combine all but six of the orange slices with the lemon juice and Grand Marnier. Cover and refrigerate for about an hour.

2 Place one raspberry in 4-6 glasses. Divide the orange slices and lemon juice/liqueur combo equally among the glasses and top with sparkling wine.

INGREDIENTS

½ navel orange, cut into thin quarter-moon slices

2 tablespoons fresh-squeezed lemon juice

¼ cup Grand Marnier

6 fresh raspberries

1 bottle (750 ml) sparkling wine, very cold

Mixed Bag

Simple enough—add wine and liquor to a bag of frozen fruit, in this case, mixed berries. A great dessert substitute!

INGREDIENTS

1½ cups frozen mixed berries (from a package), thawed

½ cup juice from thawing the berries

½ cup simple syrup (see page 88)

½ cup strawberry or blueberry vodka

1 bottle (750 ml) sparkling wine, very cold

1 In a bowl, combine the thawed fruits with the juice, simple syrup, and vodka. Cover and refrigerate for about an hour.

2 Divide the fruit/juice/syrup mixture between 4-6 glasses. Top each glass with sparkling wine. Refill as necessary.

Sweet Wine Sangrias

The nice thing about this category of sangrias is that they practically make themselves. You don't need to worry as much about whether the final mix will be sweet enough—you may, in fact, want to cut the sweetness with additional seltzer or ice.

There are sweet red wines, sweet white wines, and sweet blush wines. All of them have a ripe grape taste that brings sangria alive and, of course, is easily complemented by adding grapes. These are some of the simplest sangrias to put together. That said, they are fun to experiment with, too. Here is a range of recipes.

Strawberry Lemonade

Year in and year out, this is the most popular sangria at the Hudson-Chatham Winery's Sangria Festival in upstate New York in August. And it's frequently requested for parties under the winery tent. No wonder why—it just tastes great!

INGREDIENTS

1 bottle (750 ml) blush wine

2 cups fresh strawberries, sliced or 2 cups frozen strawberries, thawed

1 container frozen lemonade (yellow or pink)

1 container water (use the lemonade container)

Combine all ingredients in a large pitcher or container. Cover and refrigerate for four or more hours. Add ice, stir and serve.

Pink and Perky

Raspberries in blush wine can be almost too sweet. A few slices of lime temper that inclination, and add great color and cheer.

Combine all ingredients except the soda in a large pitcher or container. Cover and refrigerate for four or more hours. Add ice and soda. Stir and serve.

INGREDIENTS

1 bottle (750 ml) blush wine

1 cup raspberries, frozen

½ lime, sliced into quarter-moon slivers

1 12 oz. can lemon-lime soda

Porch Swing

A porch swing is luxurious and lazy, and so is this sangria. If you're lucky enough to enjoy a glass of it in an actual porch swing, you'll soon be asking someone else to get you a refill.

INGREDIENTS

1 bottle (750 ml) blush wine

1 large peach, pitted and cut into bite-sized pieces, frozen

1 Granny Smith apple, cored and seeded, and cut into bite-sized pieces

½ cup apple vodka

1 cup seltzer

Combine all ingredients except the seltzer in a large pitcher or container. Cover and refrigerate for four or more hours. Add ice and seltzer. Stir and serve.

Colors of Sunset

The bright cherries and sparkling slivers of lemon in this pink wine sangria do create a sunset effect. Try it and see!

Combine all ingredients except the soda in a large pitcher or container. Cover and refrigerate for four or more hours. Add ice and soda. Stir and serve.

INGREDIENTS

1 bottle (750 ml) blush wine

1 cup cherries, pitted and halved, frozen

1 lemon, sliced into half-moon slivers

½ cup gin

1 12 oz. can black cherry soda

4th of July

This is red, white, and blue, and cause for celebration! Go ahead and double the recipe; you'll be glad you did.

INGREDIENTS

1 bottle (750 ml) sweet white wine

½ cup blueberries, frozen

½ cup blackberries, frozen

½ cup cherries, pitted and halved, frozen

½ cup vodka

1 cup berry seltzer

Sliced apple cut into stars, for garnish (optional)

Combine all ingredients except the seltzer in a large pitcher or container. Cover and refrigerate for four or more hours. Add ice and seltzer. Garnish with apple stars, stir, and serve.

Variation: Although cherries certainly give this sangria a bit of an "as American as cherry pie" kind of feel, this drink is just as delicious when made with raspberries or strawberries.

Blue Lagoon

The Curaçao in this sangria turns it a great shade of tropical blue, and the watermelon pieces turn almost purple. What fun!

Combine all ingredients except the seltzer in a large pitcher or container. Cover and refrigerate for four or more hours. Add ice and seltzer. Stir and serve.

INGREDIENTS

1 bottle (750 ml) sweet white wine

2 cups bite-sized watermelon pieces, frozen

½ cup Curaçao liqueur

2 cups plain or watermelon seltzer

Basil-Dew Delight

This sangria needs advance preparation as the basil-infused vodka takes a few days. But it's worth it!

BASIL-INFUSED VODKA INGREDIENTS

1 cup vodka

½ cup loosely packed basil leaves, fresh

SANGRIA INGREDIENTS

1 bottle (750 ml) sweet white wine

2 cups bite-sized honeydew melon pieces, frozen

1 cup seltzer

Fresh basil for garnish, if desired

1 Make the basil-infused vodka: In a mason jar with a tight-fitting lid, place the basil leaves and pour in the vodka. Secure the lid and shake gently for a couple of minutes. Put the jar in the refrigerator and shake it gently once or twice a day for at least two, but up to four, days, depending on how strong you want the basil flavor to be. I like to let it sit for four days. After four days, remove the basil leaves and strain into another jar with a tight-fitting lid. Keep refrigerated until ready to use.

2 Combine ½ cup of the basil-infused vodka with all ingredients except the seltzer in a large pitcher or container. Cover and refrigerate for two or more hours. Add ice and seltzer. Stir and serve, garnishing with basil leaves if desired.

Ahhh So Good

There's nothing like a ripe pear. Unless it's in a glass of sweet wine with a ripe nectarine. A splash of lime helps them sing, and you'll be tapping your foot to the goodness of this one.

Combine all ingredients except the seltzer in a large pitcher or container. Cover and refrigerate for four or more hours. Add ice and seltzer. Stir and serve.

INGREDIENTS

1 bottle (750 ml) sweet white wine

2 nectarines, pitted and cut into bite-sized pieces, frozen

1 pear, cored and cut into bite-sized pieces, frozen

Juice from ½ lime

2 cups seltzer

Classic Sweetie

YIELD: 4-6 SERVINGS

This is a take on classic red wine sangria, but it's made with sweet red wine (the Barefoot Sweet Red is perfect for this one). This is a party pleaser, too, so have extras of all ingredients on hand.

INGREDIENTS

1 bottle (750 ml) sweet red wine

1 apple, cored and cut into bite-sized pieces

½ orange, cut into half-moon slivers

¼ cup brandy

2 cups seltzer

Combine all ingredients except the seltzer in a large pitcher or container. Cover and refrigerate for four or more hours. Add ice and seltzer. Stir and serve.

What's Love Got To Do With It?

Throw this sangria together, and no one will care. It's lovely, luscious, and light and goes down easy. If you want to get exotic, add a dash of cinnamon.

Combine all ingredients except the soda in a large pitcher or container. Cover and refrigerate for four or more hours. Add ice and soda. Stir and serve.

INGREDIENTS

1 bottle (750 ml) sweet red wine

1 nectarine, pitted and cut into bite-sized pieces

1 plum, pitted and cut into bite-sized pieces

½ cup seedless green grapes, halved

¼ cup vodka

1 12 oz. can lemon-lime soda

Rosé and Frozen Sangrias

But wait, there's more! Rosé is very popular these days, and it, too, makes a lovely sangria. Rosé is essentially a red wine that's been deliberately made into a white-style wine. Depending on the grape used, it will have the fruity character of the red wine grape of its origin, with a very light color. According to *Wine Maker Magazine*, "There are three main methods of making rosé. The principle behind rosé is developing some color in the juice. All red grapes ... have white juice. Through some form of skin contact, the anthocyanins—which compose the red or purple color in the skins—are extracted into the juice." The Spanish name for it is *rosada*, and the World Wine Guys tell me that it's popular there, too. It's got the complexity of a red with the simplicity of a white, and, served chilled, can be paired with the heavier foods that are more typically paired with red wines.

The nuances of rosé make it fun to play with when crafting sangrias. It is its own wine, and doesn't necessarily substitute well for white or red.

On the other end of the sangria spectrum is the increasingly popular sangria slushy, or frozen sangria. The concept is great, the flavor is great—it's keeping it frozen that's the trick. Like other frozen cocktails, it should be served straight out of the blender, so it's not a typical "punch" the way sangria is intended. But since it is a fun take on sangria, there are a few recipes for it, too.

Maureen's Rosé

A great friend who loves sangrias sent me this recipe, knowing I would love the cucumber in it. It's so refreshing, and just right for rosé. You do need to marinate the cucumber in the wine overnight, so keep this in mind.

INGREDIENTS

1 bottle (750 ml) dry rosé

½ cucumber, peeled and sliced into long wedges

2 teaspoons fresh-squeezed lemon juice

2 tablespoons St-Germain liqueur

1 Open the bottle of rosé and slide the cucumber pieces inside. Put the cork back in the bottle and refrigerate overnight.

2 Strain the wine into a pitcher, cutting up half the marinated cucumber into bite-sized pieces and discarding the rest. Put the cut pieces in the wine. Add the lemon juice and St-Germain. Stir and serve over ice.

Salsa-Gria

There's a really yummy salsa made with pineapple, cilantro, jalapeño, and fresh corn. It's summery and spicy and delightfully different. This sangria is similar and has everything but the corn. Serve with corn chips for a flavor combo treat.

1 Make the simple syrup: In a small saucepan, combine the water and sugar. Cook over medium heat, while stirring, until sugar is dissolved. Remove from heat and add cilantro. Cover the saucepan and let sit for several hours. Remove the leaves and strain the liquid so that there are no solids. Put the syrup in a jar, cover it, and refrigerate until cool.

2 In a large pitcher, combine the wine, pineapple pieces, pineapple juice, lime juice, jalapeño slices, ½ cup cilantro simple syrup, and tequila. Stir and refrigerate for about two hours. When ready to serve, stir in seltzer and ice.

CILANTRO SIMPLE SYRUP INGREDIENTS

1 cup water

1 cup sugar

1 cup fresh cilantro leaves (stems removed)

SANGRIA INGREDIENTS

1 bottle (750 ml) dry rosé wine

1 cup pineapple pieces, cut into bite-sized pieces

1 cup pineapple juice

1 lime, juiced

1 jalapeño, sliced thin (optional)

½ cup tequila

1 cup seltzer

Basil-Berry

Strawberries pair really well with basil, which has a slight licorice flavor. Basil is also plentiful in the summer, so make a double batch of basil simple syrup and add it to all kinds of cocktails.

BASIL SIMPLE SYRUP INGREDIENTS

1 cup water

1 cup sugar

1 cup fresh basil leaves, plus more for garnish

SANGRIA INGREDIENTS

1 bottle (750 ml) dry rosé wine

1 cup sliced fresh strawberries

1 cup berry vodka

2 cups strawberry sparkling water

1 Make the simple syrup: In a small saucepan, combine the water and sugar. Cook over medium heat, while stirring, until sugar is dissolved. Remove from heat and add basil. Cover the saucepan and let sit for several hours. Remove the leaves and strain the liquid so that there are no solids. Put the syrup in a jar, cover it, and refrigerate.

2 In a large pitcher, combine ½ cup of the simple syrup with all ingredients except the seltzer. Cover and refrigerate for about two hours. When ready to serve, stir in ice and seltzer, garnish with basil.

Peachy Sangria

I'm a sucker for herb-infused simple syrup in rosé sangria, so here's another iteration, with peaches and sage. So yummy! Make the simple syrup the day or night before so it's ready when you want to put the sangria together.

1 Make the simple syrup: In a small saucepan, combine the water and sugar. Cook over medium heat, while stirring, until sugar is dissolved. Remove from heat and add sage. Cover the saucepan and let sit for several hours. Remove the leaves and strain the liquid so that there are no solids. Put the syrup in a jar, cover it, and refrigerate. The syrup will keep in the refrigerator, tightly sealed, for up to two weeks.

2 In a large pitcher, combine all ingredients except the seltzer. Cover and refrigerate for about two hours. When ready to serve, stir in ice and seltzer.

SAGE SIMPLE SYRUP INGREDIENTS

1 cup water

1 cup sugar

About 1 cup (30-40) fresh sage leaves

SANGRIA INGREDIENTS

1 bottle (750 ml) dry rosé wine

2 peaches, pitted and cut into bite-sized pieces

½ cup brandy

1 cup seltzer

½ cup sage simple syrup

Minty Melon

Here's another variation on an herb-infused rosé-gria—this one with watermelon (soooo good) and fresh mint (ahhh!). Seriously, double the recipe right away. Make the simple syrup the day or night before so it's ready when you want to put the sangria together.

MINT SIMPLE SYRUP INGREDIENTS

1 cup water

1 cup sugar

1 cup fresh mint leaves

SANGRIA INGREDIENTS

1 bottle (750 ml) dry rosé wine

2 cups bite-sized watermelon pieces, frozen

½ cup tequila

6-8 large mint leaves

1 cup watermelon sparkling water

½ cup mint simple syrup

1 Make the simple syrup: In a small saucepan, combine the water and sugar. Cook over medium heat, while stirring, until sugar is dissolved. Remove from heat and add mint. Cover the saucepan and let sit for several hours. Remove the leaves and strain the liquid so that there are no solids. Put the syrup in a jar, cover it, and refrigerate. The syrup will keep in the refrigerator, tightly sealed, for up to two weeks.

2 In a large pitcher, combine all ingredients except the sparkling water. Cover and refrigerate for about two hours. When ready to serve, stir in ice and sparkling water.

Fro-Loupe-a-Gria

The delicate flavor of cantaloupe is perfect for frozen sangria. A splash of lime, and a splash of raspberry certainly help, too!

1 In a 4-cup measuring cup, combine the liqueur and sugar. Stir until sugar is dissolved.

2 Put all other ingredients in a blender or food processor. Turn on high and pulverize until ingredients are slushy. Add the raspberry sugar mixture and pulse to combine. Distribute among glasses, and garnish with a lime wedge and raspberries if desired.

INGREDIENTS

½ cup raspberry liqueur

½ cup sugar

1 bottle (750 ml) light-bodied dry white wine

6 cups bite-sized pieces fresh cantaloupe, frozen

Juice of 1 lime

1 cup ice

Lime slices for garnish, if desired

Fresh raspberries for garnish, if desired

Slush Berry

YIELD: 4-6 SERVINGS

Loads and loads of berries make this almost as healthy as it is tasty! Perfect on a summer night with BBQ.

INGREDIENTS

1 bottle (750 ml) sweet red wine

1 cup blueberries

1 cup raspberries

1 cup strawberries

1 cup orange juice

¼ cup Triple Sec

1 cup (or more) ice

Combine all ingredients except the ice in a large bowl. Stir to combine. Process the fruit and wine in batches until it is a slurry. Put a cup of ice in the blender and add the fruit slurry. Pulverize on high until everything is combined and slushy. Divide among glasses and serve.

Frozen Berry-Ade Sangria

YIELD: 4-6 SERVINGS

You'll need ice cube trays for this one, which make the actual prep very easy as you just use frozen cubes, add wine and fruit, and blend.

1 Fill one ice cube tray with wine and another with lemonade. Put the trays in the freezer and wait until the liquids are frozen solid, four to six hours or overnight.

2 Add the wine and lemonade cubes to a blender along with the strawberries, rum, and any wine left in the bottle. Pulverize until combined. Divide among glasses, and garnish each with a slice of lemon or lime.

INGREDIENTS

1 bottle (750 ml) sweet white or blush wine

2 cups lemonade

1 cup fresh strawberries, sliced

½ cup dark rum

Thin lemon or lime slices for garnish

Cheater-grias

I don't know what rock I've been living under the past few years, but I hadn't realized until I started working on this book how many flavored juices, sodas, seltzers, sparkling waters, flavored malt beverages and—wow!—SpikedSeltzers™ there are on the market now. Finding this explosion of flavored beverages when you're dreaming up sangria recipes is like going from the basic 24-pack of Crayola™ crayons to the "ultimate" collection of 152 different colors when your assignment is to draw a picture of paradise. Choices, choices!

And as if the concept of sangria isn't simple enough—wine, fruit, booze, a sweetener, some bubbles—this wealth of exotic juice combinations and flavored waters just made coming up with something delicious even easier. I've called this chapter Cheater-grias because, well, that's what these recipes are. No need to refrigerate overnight, just stir and serve. Play with these and you'll be inspired to experiment, too. Challenge your entourage to a cheater-gria party where everyone brings their own combo, and see whose you like best.

Cheater-gridients

Let's start with fruit juice combinations. These are in the refrigerated section near the orange juice, grapefruit juice, and lemonade. Tropicana™ now makes four different lemonades, including peach lemonade. Their watermelon juice is everywhere, and they've introduced strawberry-peach and pineapple-mango with lime. They have a new "probiotics" line that includes peach passion fruit,

and a "farmstand" line that includes pomegranate-blueberry (a classic sangria combo!). Tropicana's "Twisters"™ are juices hopped up with sugar, but adding red wine, ice, and a splash of vodka to the Cherry Berry Blast sounds like a great summer punch. Welch's™ is right there, too; in fact, they have Red Sangria and White Sangria juice combos—ha! Or try their juice "cocktails" that are available in a carton or frozen and include combos like apple/grape/cherry, white grape/peach, raspberry/lime, or berry/pineapple/passion fruit, which they call "Paradise in a Glass." There are loads of mocktail recipes on Welch's™ website, too. Fun!

Bai™ is a relative newcomer to the juice world, but is another inspiration if your ultimate goal is tasty sangria. They describe what they're up to as part of a "bevolution"—"A world of beverages without borders—with no limits on taste, geography or imagination." OK. Their line is where you'll find Sumatra Dragonfruit, Ipanema Pomegranate, or Andes Coconut Lime. Toss in red, white, sparkling, or sweet wine and you're on to something.

But wait—there are flavored waters, too! Sanavi™ is a line of sparkling spring waters that proudly boast "only 2 ingredients"—water from Vermont and an organic, natural flavor (lemon, lime, blueberry, strawberry, coconut, and orange mango, for now). Hint™ water—which claims to be the best-selling all-natural flavored water—has a line of Hint Fizz flavors, including watermelon and blackberry. Sanavi™, anyone? Hint, Hint. Look in this chapter for recipes with these.

This book would need 101 more recipes to be able to include combos with all the flavors of seltzer and soda that are available these days. And last but not least, there are SpikedSeltzers™—made by fermenting natural citrus extracts and sugars to produce these drinks with 6% alcohol. Introduced in 2013 (see, where have I been?!?), these beautifully packaged beverages come in grapefruit, lime, cranberry, and orange flavors.

Cheatin' Easy

Oh, so easy! These ingredients were made for each other, and for sangria.

INGREDIENTS

1 bottle (750 ml) fruity dry red wine (like a Beaujolais or Pinot Noir)

2 cups berry/pineapple/passionfruit juice

1 cup frozen blueberries

¼ cup berry vodka

1 17 oz. bottle Sanavi™ Lime sparkling water

Combine all ingredients in a pitcher. Stir and serve over ice.

184 Cheater-grias

Cheatin' Heart

The deep red wine and deep red pomegranate-blueberry juice give a great impression of, well, blood. If you're feeling blue or maybe used, or just in a mood, throw this together.

Combine all ingredients in a pitcher. Stir and serve over ice.

INGREDIENTS

1 bottle (750 ml) bold dry red (like a California Merlot)

1 12 oz. bottle pomegranate-blueberry juice

1 cup sliced fresh strawberries

¼ cup vodka

2 cups blueberry seltzer

Spiked Nice

We do live in a bevrolution, and the flavors that can be tried are mouth-watering, as you'll discover when you put these ingredients together.

INGREDIENTS

1 bottle (750 ml) bold dry red (like a Spanish Tempranillo)

2 fresh peaches, pitted and cut into bite-sized pieces, or 1½ cups frozen peach slices, cut in half

1 12 oz. can of SpikedSeltzer™ Cape Cod Cranberry

¼ cup tequila

1 lime or lemon, cut into small wedges

Combine the wine, fruit and SpikedSeltzer™ in a pitcher. Pour into glasses filled with ice, and garnish with a lime or lemon wedge.

Hint, Hint

Ok, this is a big wet kiss to Hint™ sparkling water, but so be it. They're good, and the blackberry is perfect in this sangria.

Combine all ingredients in a pitcher and stir.
Serve over ice.

INGREDIENTS

1 bottle (750 ml) light-bodied dry red wine (like a Pinot Noir)

2 cups strawberry-raspberry juice

1 cup fresh or frozen raspberries

1 16.9 oz. bottle Hint™ Fizz Blackberry sparkling water

Passionate Cheat

Passion fruit sounds good, doesn't it? And it tastes good. But it's a pain to slice and eat fresh. How wonderful that it's in so many juice combinations! This one marries it with peaches and oranges.

INGREDIENTS

1 bottle (750 ml) dry white wine

2 cups peach-passion fruit juice

½ cup Triple Sec or Grand Marnier

2 cups peach sparkling water

Orange slices for garnish

Combine wine, juice, Triple Sec, and sparkling water in a pitcher. Stir and serve over ice. Garnish glasses with orange slices.

Apple of My Cheating Eye

I know, I know, I'm having way too much fun with the names of these sangrias! What's even more fun is experimenting with the almost instant flavors and enjoying them with friends.

Combine all ingredients in a pitcher. Stir and serve over ice.

INGREDIENTS

1 bottle (750 ml) dry white wine

2 cups orange-pineapple-apple juice

1 apple, cored and cut into bite-sized pieces

½ cup Triple Sec

2 cups green apple seltzer

Caught Red-handed

YIELD: 4-6 SERVINGS

Yes, there are even packaged fruits with hot stuff on them! Chili-lime mango chunks are one of them, and making engaging sangria with them is simple: accentuate the sweet, spicy, and slightly sour, and serve over ice. Nice!

INGREDIENTS

1 bottle (750 ml) dry white wine

1 12 oz. bag chili-lime mango chunks

1 cup Mango Twist juice

½ cup gin

2 cups lime seltzer

1 lime, cut into wedges

Combine all ingredients except the seltzer in a pitcher. Let it sit for about an hour (no need to refrigerate). Stir in seltzer and serve over ice. Garnish glasses with lime wedges.

Cheating on the Beach

If you haven't done it yet, now's the time. 'Nuff said.

Combine all ingredients in a pitcher. Stir and serve over ice. Garnish each glass with a Maraschino cherry if desired.

INGREDIENTS

1 bottle (750 ml) dry white wine

2 cups canned or fresh bite-sized pineapple pieces

½ cup dark rum

2 cups coconut sparkling water

Maraschino cherries for garnish, if desired

This is Nuts

YIELD: 4-6 SERVINGS

Turns out hazelnut is a great complement to orange. This sangria brings them together and drives them home with a can of SpikedSeltzer™ Valencia Orange. Wow.

INGREDIENTS

1 bottle (750 ml) dry white wine

1 large orange, sliced into thin half-moons, some reserved for garnish

½ cup Frangelico or hazelnut liqueur

1 12 oz. can SpikedSeltzer™ Valencia Orange

Combine all ingredients in a pitcher. Stir and serve over ice. Garnish glasses with orange slices if desired.

Cheatin' Down Under

Serve this at your next party, and everyone will be heading down under for some serious fun. Strawberries, kiwis, vodka, and sparkling wine. The only other thing you need is barbeque.

Combine all ingredients in a pitcher. Stir gently and serve over ice, dividing the strawberries evenly among the glasses.

INGREDIENTS

1 bottle (750 ml) semi-dry sparkling wine

1½ cups fresh strawberries, sliced

2 cups strawberry-kiwi juice

½ cup vodka

Sangrias for a Crowd

As a punch, sangria is intended to be drunk by a crowd. When I talked to Mike and Jeff, the World Wine Guys, they said what I thought was the truest thing I'd ever heard about sangria: "It goes quickly," they noted. "Have another set of ingredients and a bowl of pre-sliced fruit on hand because you are going to be making a second batch. Better yet, have a third backup ready to go, as well."

Sangria is fruity and fun. Sangria makes people happy. Sangria is versatile—it can be served with appetizers, with a main course (especially grilled meats or, if you're lucky, paella), and it can be served with dessert; in fact, it can BE dessert since it's fruit and wine! A plate of cookies and brownies is an excellent accompaniment, though.

This chapter contains eight sangria recipes that make about three gallons each. Given that a glass of sangria will measure out to about eight ounces with the fruit and other ingredients, that's enough for about 48 glasses. If you figure 2-3 glasses per person, these crowd-sized sangrias should satisfy a party of a couple dozen folks. One thing I've found when making sangria for the Hudson-Chatham Winery's annual sangria festival is that, when you notice the liquid going down, you can supplement it without adding more fruit. So be sure to have extra wine, juice, seltzer, and booze on hand to boost the recipes if necessary. And if you happen to have leftovers, remove some of the fruit so that the proportion is about 50-50 fruit and liquid, and refrigerate it. Add more seltzer when serving. It's only good for another day or two, so drink up!

TIP: USE TWO EQUAL-SIZED PITCHERS TO START THESE SANGRIAS, AS THEY ARE EASY TO FIT INTO THE REFRIGERATOR. IT'S MUCH MORE DIFFICULT TO FIT A PUNCH BOWL!

Classic Red Wine Sangria I

YIELD: 24 SERVINGS

For this recipe, I suggest using a dry but bigger-bodied red. Something Spanish. The World Wine Guys (who live in Spain for part of the year) often recommend Tempranillo. This is a jammy red with deep fruit notes. Citrus complements this flavor profile really well.

INGREDIENTS

5 apples, cored and seeded, cut into bite-sized pieces

5 oranges, sliced into quarter-moon slivers (seeds removed)

4 cups (32 oz.) pomegranate juice

½ cup pomegranate seeds

1½ cups brandy

12 bottles Spanish dry red wine

6 cups (48 oz.) lemon-lime soda

1 Divide the pieces of fruit equally between the pitchers. Add two cups of pomegranate juice to each pitcher and stir. Add ¾ cup of brandy to each pitcher. Next, add four bottles of wine to the pitchers (you'll add the other bottles when you combine the pitchers). Stir all these ingredients together, cover the pitchers with plastic wrap or foil, and refrigerate overnight.

2 An hour before the sangria is to be served, combine the two pitchers into a large punch bowl. Add the remaining four bottles of wine and stir. Cover the punch bowl and place it in a cool spot. When you're ready to serve the sangria, slowly add the soda and gently stir it so you don't lose too much of the soda's carbonation. Serve with lots of ice on the side so that guests can fill their glasses as they see fit, and then ladle the sangria into the glass.

Classic Red Wine Sangria II

YIELD: 24 SERVINGS

This recipe uses a lighter-bodied dry red wine so that the fruits don't get overwhelmed. A Pinot Noir from Washington, Oregon, or New York—which is typically light-bodied, subtle, and with a bright fruit note on the finish—is a great choice.

1 Divide the pieces of fruit equally between the pitchers. Add two cups of apple juice and one cup of peach nectar to each pitcher and stir. Add ¼ cup of brandy to each pitcher. Next, add four bottles of wine to each of the pitchers (you'll add the other bottles when you combine the pitchers). Stir all these ingredients together, cover the pitchers with plastic wrap or foil, and refrigerate overnight.

2 An hour before the sangria is to be served, combine the two pitchers into a large punch bowl. Add the remaining four bottles of wine and stir. Cover the punch bowl and place it in a cool spot. When you're ready to serve the sangria, slowly add the seltzer and gently stir it so you don't lose too much of the carbonation. Serve with lots of ice on the side so that guests can fill their glasses as they see fit, and then ladle the sangria into the glass.

INGREDIENTS

- 4 cups seedless red grapes, halved
- 5 apples, cored and cut into bite-sized pieces
- 4 ripe peaches, pitted and cut into bite-sized pieces
- 4 cups apple juice (not cider)
- 2 cups peach nectar
- ½ cup brandy
- 12 bottles light-bodied dry red wine
- 6 cups (48 oz.) plain seltzer

Classic Red Wine Sangria III

YIELD: 24 SERVINGS

Finally, a party sangria that combines a dry red and a sweet red. My suggestion is a Spanish red like a Garnacha and, for a sweet red, a Lambrusco. This combo will give you strong berry notes, which complement a berry-oriented sangria.

INGREDIENTS

3 cups fresh or frozen strawberries, halved, juice reserved

3 cups fresh or frozen blueberries

2 cups fresh or frozen blackberries

1 cup brandy

6 bottles dry red wine

6 bottles sweet red wine

6 cups plain or unsweetened berry seltzer, or 3 cups of each

1 Divide the fruit equally between the pitchers. Divide the juice from the frozen strawberries between the pitchers. Add ½ cup of brandy to each pitcher and stir. Next, add four bottles of wine to each of the pitchers (you'll add the other bottles when you combine the pitchers). Stir all these ingredients together, cover the pitchers with plastic wrap or foil, and refrigerate overnight.

2 An hour before the sangria is to be served, combine the two pitchers into a large punch bowl. Add the remaining four bottles of wine and stir. Cover the punch bowl and place it in a cool spot. When you're ready to serve the sangria, slowly add the seltzer and gently stir it so you don't lose too much of the carbonation. Serve with lots of ice on the side so that guests can fill their glasses as they see fit, and then ladle the sangria into the glass.

Sangria Blanca

As with the red wine sangria recipes, these variations will play with different styles of the dry wines—this one will feature a light-bodied, citrus-y white. Choose a relatively inexpensive Pinot Grigio. The fruit will really stand out in this and it won't be too sweet.

1 Divide the pieces of fruit equally between the pitchers. Add 1½ cups of peach nectar and one cup of apple juice to each pitcher and stir. Add ¾ cup of raspberry liqueur to each pitcher. Next, add four bottles of wine to each of the pitchers (you'll add the other bottles when you combine the pitchers). Stir all these ingredients together, cover the pitcher with plastic wrap or foil, and refrigerate overnight.

2 An hour before the sangria is to be served, combine the two pitchers into a large punch bowl. Add the remaining four bottles of wine and stir. Cover the punch bowl and place it in a cool spot. When you're ready to serve the sangria, slowly add the seltzer and gently stir it so you don't lose too much of the carbonation. Serve with lots of ice on the side so that guests can fill their glasses as they see fit, and then ladle the sangria into the glass.

INGREDIENTS

- 6 peaches, pitted and cut into bite-sized pieces
- 2 Granny Smith apples, cored and cut into bite-sized pieces
- 2 cups fresh or frozen raspberries
- 3 cups peach nectar
- 2 cups apple juice (not cider)
- 1½ cups raspberry liqueur
- 12 bottles light-bodied dry white wine
- 6 cups plain seltzer

Mas Sangria Blanca

YIELD: 24 SERVINGS

This recipe uses a fruitier dry white. A Spanish Albariño is a good selection, or even an oaked Chardonnay. Because the wine itself will have more notes of vanilla, ripe melon, or even honey, the fruit selection includes lots of bright citrus.

INGREDIENTS

6 oranges, sliced into thin half-moons

4 lemons, sliced into thin half-moons

3 limes, sliced into thin half-moons

1 cup brandy

12 bottles fruity dry white wine

6 cups lemon-lime soda

1 Divide the pieces of fruit equally between the pitchers, including the juice that's generated from slicing the fruits. Add ½ cup of brandy to each pitcher. Next, add four bottles of wine to each of the pitchers (you'll add the other bottles when you combine the pitchers). Stir all these ingredients together, cover the pitchers with plastic wrap or foil, and refrigerate overnight.

2 An hour before the sangria is to be served, combine the two pitchers into a large punch bowl. Add the remaining four bottles of wine and stir. Cover the punch bowl and place it in a cool spot. When you're ready to serve the sangria, slowly add the soda and gently stir it so you don't lose too much of the carbonation. Serve with lots of ice on the side so that guests can fill their glasses as they see fit, and then ladle the sangria into the glass.

Sangria Blanca Tropica

Tropical fruits are great for white wine sangrias, and they definitely please any crowd. This sangria showcases pineapple, kiwi, and red grapefruit. Freeze the kiwi pieces before putting them in the sangria, as this will help them hold up better. A fruitier white is best with this, too—a Viognier is excellent, but you could also use a fruitier Sauvignon Blanc. Ask your local wine store for a recommendation.

1 Put two cups pineapple chunks in each pitcher and divide the grapefruit pieces evenly between them. Add ½ cup of rum to each pitcher and stir. Next, add four bottles of wine to each of the pitchers (you'll add the other bottles when you combine the pitchers), and stir all these ingredients together. Add one cup of kiwi pieces to each pitcher and gently press them into the sangria. Cover the pitchers with plastic wrap or foil and refrigerate overnight. Put the extra cup of kiwi pieces in a plastic baggie and freeze them.

2 An hour before the sangria is to be served, combine the two pitchers into a large punch bowl. Add the remaining four bottles of wine and the bag of frozen kiwi pieces, and stir. Cover the punch bowl and place it in a cool spot. When you're ready to serve the sangria, slowly add the seltzer and gently stir it so you don't lose too much of the carbonation. Serve with lots of ice on the side so that guests can fill their glasses as they see fit, and then ladle the sangria into the glass.

INGREDIENTS

4 cups fresh or frozen pineapple chunks

3 large red grapefruits, peeled, wedges cut into bite-sized pieces

1 cup dark rum

12 bottles fruity, dry white wine

3 cups bite-sized kiwi pieces from fresh, peeled kiwis, frozen

6 cups plain seltzer

Summer Day Strawberry Sangria

YIELD: 24 SERVINGS

Not only is this a delicious sangria, it is also very pretty. The bright red strawberry pieces and slices of bright yellow lemon swim in a cotton-candy pink wine. Everyone loves this sangria. It's especially perfect for occasions when the girls gather, like bridal and baby showers.

INGREDIENTS

4 containers frozen lemonade (pink or yellow, though pink is preferable)

2 lemons, sliced into very thin half-moons

6 cups fresh strawberries, sliced thin

12 bottles sweet blush wine

6 cups plain seltzer

1 Place two containers of frozen lemonade in each pitcher, adding two containers of water to each to dilute the lemonade. Stir. Divide the lemon and strawberry slices equally between the two pitchers. Next, add four bottles of wine to each of the pitchers (you'll add the other bottles when you combine the pitchers). Stir, cover the pitchers with plastic wrap or foil, and refrigerate overnight.

2 An hour before the sangria is to be served, combine the two pitchers into a large punch bowl. Add the remaining four bottles of wine and stir. Cover the punch bowl and place it in a cool spot. When you're ready to serve the sangria, slowly add the seltzer and gently stir it so you don't lose too much of the carbonation. Serve with lots of ice on the side so that guests can fill their glasses as they see fit, and then ladle the sangria into the glass.

Memorable Moscato-Gria

This is a celebration sangria, for sure, as it uses Moscato d'Asti, a sweet and economically priced alternative to Prosecco or other sparkling wine. Because it's bubbly, it gets added to the marinated fruit just before serving, which is a slight variation from more traditional sangria. The results, however, are impressive and delicious.

1 In a large bowl, combine the nectarine pieces, raspberries, and lime juice. Stir gently to combine. Pour the Grand Marnier over the fruit, cover, and refrigerate overnight.

2 Transfer the marinated fruit to a large punch bowl. Add the Moscato d'Asti, pouring the bottles gently and from the side so that it stays bubbly. Serve with lots of ice.

INGREDIENTS

6 nectarines, pitted and cut into bite-sized pieces

4 cups raspberries

Juice of 2 limes

1½ cups Grand Marnier

12 bottles Moscato d'Asti

Index

ABOUT THE AUTHOR

As an owner of the Hudson-Chatham Winery in New York's Hudson Valley, Dominique DeVito has staged an annual Sangria Festival for the past decade. The festival features fresh-made sangrias, which she and her team develop every year. That experience has helped her understand how fun—and forgiving—sangria can be. All you need is fruit, wine, spirits, and friends, and you have a party. Dominique traveled extensively in Spain as a child and loves every opportunity to think about the country that gave the world the greatest wine cocktail of them all. *Viva Sangria!*

ABOUT CIDER MILL PRESS BOOK PUBLISHERS

Good ideas ripen with time. From seed to harvest, Cider Mill
Press brings fine reading, information, and entertainment
together between the covers of its creatively crafted books.
Our Cider Mill bears fruit twice a year, publishing
a new crop of titles each spring and fall.

"Where Good Books Are Ready for Press"
501 Nelson Place
Nashville, Tennessee 37214

cidermillpress.com